MARSHALL
of
CAMBRIDGE

MARSHALL
of
CAMBRIDGE

Stephen Skinner

TEMPUS

By the same author

BAC One-Eleven – The Whole Story (Tempus Publishing, 2002)

Frontispiece: This photograph sums up the immense activity that Marshall put into the 1982 Falkland Campaign – fitting the Hercules with a flight-refuelling probe and then fitting tanker capability. *(Paul Greenaway)*

Front cover: RAF Hercules over Port Stanley, Falkland Islands *(Paul Greenaway)*
Back cover: Lockheed TriStar civil freighter conversion, N306GB, for Arrow Air. *(MA)*
Back cover logo: The Marshall coat of arms. The motto is 'Felix qui laborat' which translates as 'Happy is he who works'. *(MA)*

First published 2003

Tempus Publishing Limited
The Mill, Brimscombe Port,
Stroud, Gloucestershire, GL5 2QG

© Stephen Skinner, 2003

British Library Cataloguing in Publication Data.
A catalogue record for this book is available from the British Library.

ISBN 0 7524 3125 0

Typesetting and origination by Tempus Publishing Limited
Printed in Great Britain by Midway Colour Print, Wiltshire

Contents

Michael Marshall, Chairman of Marshall Group, together with his father, Sir Arthur, Honorary Life President in December 1989. Michael Marshall was then (and still is) Deputy Lieutenant of Cambridgeshire and Sir Arthur was High Sheriff. *(MA)*

Foreword

I was delighted when I heard from Stephen Skinner that he wanted to compile an exciting, illustrated history of Marshall Aerospace to show the major contribution which Marshall of Cambridge has made to aviation during its seventy-four years of activities at its Cambridge Airport.

We in the Marshall of Cambridge Group of companies are proud of our history as a private family-owned company during the years following our foundation in the retail motor business by my grandfather in 1909. We have grown into a group of companies with combined annual sales of £500 million, with a strong ethos of staff loyalty and training and a focus on providing our customers with exceptional service and value for money.

We are proud of the entrepreneurial courage and enthusiasm of my grandfather, and of my father's energy and love of aviation which enabled the company to play such a vital role in the development of flying training before and during the Second World War, and to become the predominant aircraft repair centre during the war. After the war it was to become the sub-contractor to most of the British aircraft companies, before they were merged together into what is now BAE SYSTEMS. We have subsequently supported the RAF on aircraft which were purchased from the United States. Marshall's work on C-130 Hercules started in 1965, and the company has since gone on to support this aircraft type for many air forces and operators from all over the world. To date it has completed over 600 modifications on the RAF's C-130s and is probably best known for its work during the Falklands Crisis, during which we designed and fitted the flight-refuelling installation which enabled the C-130s to fly to the Falkland Islands within twenty-one days of the conversion being first requested! The contract to convert TriStars into tankers and freighters was won the following year.

Marshall is proud of the part it has played on both the national and international aviation scene, and also for the close relationship that it has developed with Cambridge University and City.

It is appropriate that this book is being published in this centennial year of aviation, which incidentally coincides with the centennial year of my father, who was born just thirteen days prior to the first powered flight by the Wright Brothers at Kitty Hawk on 17 December 1903. During the last seventy-four of those years Marshall has played an increasingly important role, often somewhat behind the scenes, in support of the UK and world aviation industry, and this is vividly illustrated in Stephen Skinner's pictorial history.

Mr Michael Marshall CBE DL
Chairman, Marshall of Cambridge
November 2003

Preface

The story of British aviation cannot be told without paying due respect to the enterprise established by the Marshall family in Cambridge at the beginning of the last century. And since 2003 is the centenary year of flight, it is fitting to pay tribute to the business that played its part in the formative years of aviation and to record how it grew to become the thriving organisation that it is today, and one that has deservedly earned a prominent role in the city of Cambridge.

When examining the number of British types which the company has been involved with, it seems simpler to count those which are the exception and have *not* spent time in the Marshall hangars! And it is not only British aircraft that have benefited from Marshall expertise, but also many major foreign manufacturers, notably Lockheed and Boeing. The type of work carried out covers everything from design and manufacture, to refurbishment, rebuild and modification.

It is helpful to remember that the firm's origins were in the motor business and that in the early years of aviation there was a close link between motoring and flying. The company is still very heavily involved in the motor business today with large-scale motor dealerships and the manufacture of vehicle bodies. Just as over the years the company has provided aircraft to military and civilian customers, it has also provided a great number of vehicles for both military and commercial use.

Although I have sought to tell the story of the firm through its involvement in aviation, illustrated with a large number of photographs, mostly from the Marshall archives, I have included some photographs of the commercial and military vehicles in order to regularly remind the reader of their importance to the firm and its continuing prosperity. This diversity has been a strength to the Marshall Group over the decades as the country went to war and then came peace, so swords were turned into ploughshares.

This painting by Gerald Coulson was presented to Sir Arthur Marshall on his retirement in 1989. It shows a selection of the aircraft that Marshall's has worked on. The key to the painting is shown below. *(MA)*

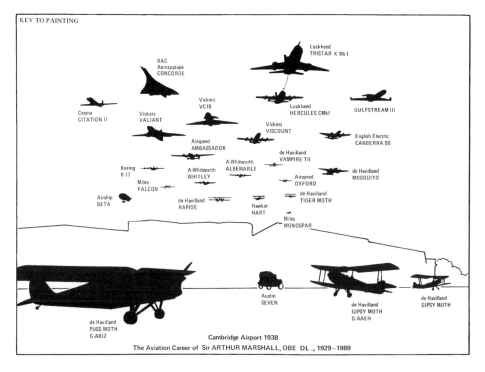

KEY TO PAINTING

Lockheed TRISTAR K Mk1

BAC Aerospatiale CONCORDE

Vickers VC10

Lockheed HERCULES CMkI

GULFSTREAM III

Cessna CITATION II

Vickers VALIANT

Vickers VISCOUNT

English Electric CANBERRA B6

Airspeed AMBASSADOR

de Havilland VAMPIRE TII

A-Whitworth ALBEMARLE

Boeing B-17

A-Whitworth WHITLEY

de Havilland MOSQUITO

Miles FALCON

Airspeed OXFORD

Airship BETA

de Havilland RAPIDE

de Havilland TIGER MOTH

Hawker HART

Miles MONOSPAR

de Havilland PUSS MOTH G-ABIZ

Austin SEVEN

de Havilland GIPSY MOTH G-AAEH

de Havilland GIPSY MOTH

Cambridge Airport 1938

The Aviation Career of Sir ARTHUR MARSHALL, OBE DL ., 1929—1989

Acknowledgements

First and foremost I would like to thank Michael Marshall, Chairman of Marshall Group, for kindly agreeing to write the foreword to this book. Special thanks are due to Terry Holloway, Group Support Executive, for the time he spent in helping me with my task. I would also like to mention Keith Ingle and his staff in Technical Publications who helped in the provision of photographs.

As ever my wife, Jane, has given me great help and editorial assistance. Finally, I thank Sir Arthur Marshall who gave up some of his time to see me and took an active interest in the publication of this book.

All photographs are from the Marshall Group (*MA* – Marshall Aerospace) except where expressly stated.

one

The Founding of the Company

The Marshall business began when David Marshall, father of Sir Arthur Marshall and grandfather of the present chairman of the company, Michael Marshall, set up a chauffeur-driven car-hire company in Brunswick Gardens, central Cambridge on 1 October 1909. Reflecting its address, the company was initially called the Brunswick Motor Car Co. but during the First World War, owing to anti-German feeling, the name was changed to Marshall's Garage.

The hire-car business quickly outgrew the restricted converted stables in Brunswick Gardens, moving around the corner to King Street and later Jesus Lane when in 1912 the company added sales and service to its portfolio. It was during that year that Marshall had their first brush with aviation when an army airship, *Beta 2*, was in trouble over the city and landed by the River Cam where its engine was repaired in the garage workshops. However, with the onset of war in August 1914, the demand for hire-car business for private use fell sharply and David Marshall then looked to employ his talents in other areas. He went to France where he was initially involved in catering at the front and later returned to the UK to manage the catering at Woolwich Arsenal, which provided 24,000 meals per day.

David Marshall was a man of vision who recognised the significance of the motor car rather earlier than many others and, with the end of the war, David Marshall saw that air travel would grow, and purchased a large, redundant Handley Page bomber. However, the bomber was never put to use and for most of the immediate post-war years the emphasis was on developing the vehicle-hire business. David Marshall obtained the Austin Distributorship for Cambridgeshire in 1920 and the company soon became agents for other manufacturers, such as Talbot, Belsize and Fiat.

Marshall's first car, a Belgian-built Metallurgique in King Street, Cambridge, in 1911. The company, then called the Brunswick Motor Car Co., started in converted stables at Brunswick Gardens in Cambridge in 1909 expanding into King Street in the following year. *(Cambridge Daily News)*

The company's first brush with aviation. The Army airship *Beta* which, suffering from engine trouble, landed in Jesus College grounds in 1912. The garage provided assistance to the Army engineers so that the airship's engine could be repaired. *(MA)*

His son, Arthur, was to have the benefit of a good education and was sent to Tonbridge School. He then became an undergraduate to read Engineering at Jesus College, Cambridge, in October 1922 and proved an exceptional athlete. Arthur Marshall was chosen as a reserve to run for Great Britain in the 1924 Paris Olympics with fellow undergraduates of Jesus College – Harold Abrahams and Eric Liddell. The story of these two and the Olympics was told in the Oscar-winning British film, *Chariots of Fire*, produced in 1981. After graduation Arthur Marshall naturally joined the family firm, selling cars at the Jesus Lane Garage.

Marshall's first aerodrome

Arthur Marshall learned to fly in 1928 and a little later purchased a Gipsy Moth, G-AAEH, directly from de Havilland's at Stag Lane Airfield, Edgware, London. Father and son then had the wisdom to buy forty-five acres of land for an aerodrome just off the Newmarket Road, between the Cambridge football club, Coldhams Brook, and approximately where the present Barnwell Road runs, only a few hundred yards west of the present airfield site. This was particularly convenient since their family home Whitehill was adjacent. The first of many hangars for Marshall was erected on site by Boulton & Paul (a Norwich-based company, later also known for the manufacture of aircraft and gun turrets).

Official openings often come rather late and such was the case with Marshall's aerodrome. It was only 'opened' on 9 June 1929: forty-three aircraft flew in, the Cambridgeshire Regimental Band played, the famous 1924 Olympic athlete Harold Abrahams was the commentator, there was a spirited flying display and pilots present included Alan Cobham and Dermot Boyle, later Marshal of the RAF. The razzmatazz of this event created much publicity and a flying school was opened in October that year and another Gipsy Moth, G-EBYZ, joined the firm. In 1930 the operation was formalised as Marshall's Flying School with Arthur giving most of the lessons and still working in the garage. With the growth in business, more flying instructors were appointed to cope with demand.

Woolwich Arsenal canteen in the First World War. David Marshall, founder of the company, was anxious to take part in the war and was involved in the catering at the front in France. Later during the war, he managed the catering at Woolwich Arsenal, which provided 24,000 meals per day. *(MA)*

The first pupil was Norman de Bruyne, then Junior Bursar of Trinity College, Cambridge. Over the years a number of dons copied his example, along with well-heeled undergraduates such as Victor Rothschild. However, those who signed up at Marshall's Flying School were not only 'gown' (i.e. the academics of Cambridge) but also the 'town' and included men who later became test pilots, for instance, Bill Humble, later wartime Chief Test Pilot of Hawkers. Later trainees were Hamish Hamilton, the publisher, and David Garnett, author and member of the Bloomsbury literati.

Other patrons of the aerodrome were the Prince of Wales, later Duke of Windsor, and three men who were to have a major effect on UK aviation: Witney Straight, Peter Masefield and Alan Cobham, who toured the country in the early 1930s with highly-entertaining 'flying circuses' to enthuse the young in all things aeronautical.

While the development of the aeronautical side of the business proceeded apace, the motor vehicle side was facing more competition as rivals appeared on the scene. Figures show that car sales increased nearly 500 per cent between 1926 and 1936. Austin were keen to promote sales and Marshall worked hard to maintain the franchise. For the 1935 Silver Jubilee three Austin 7s were displayed in patriotic red, white and blue at the Jesus Lane showrooms, but the white one had to be resprayed black before anyone would buy it! To this day, Marshall have a connection with Austin through its successor, Rover, for which they have a franchise.

Fairey 111A seaplane. This is the same type of aircraft in which David and his son Arthur Marshall made their first flights at Brighton in July 1919. *(R. T. Jackson)*

Handley Page 0/400 bomber. David Marshall purchased a surplus example of the bomber in 1919 for £5. It was not put into service but parts were used in the fabrication of a sand yacht that the Marshall family used at Heacham, Norfolk, in the 1920s. *(MA)*

Handley Page W8 G-EAPJ in which David and Arthur Marshall flew from Croydon to Paris, Le Bourget, in 1922. *(MA)*

Aircraft line-up at the ceremonial opening of the Fen Ditton aerodrome in Cambridge, only a few hundred yards west of the present company aerodrome at Teversham. *(MA)*

The approach of the Second World War and the new aerodrome

In 1934 the Cambridge Aero Club was formed, which soon expanded in 1936 to become the University Aero Club, and the serious training of the many young men eager to become pilots began. In the early 1930s an approach was made to the RAF for Fen Ditton aerodrome to become a Reserve Flying School but it was deemed too small. So the company entered into negotiations with Cambridge City Council for the acquisition of a new site which could fulfil these specifications. After much discussion and a counter proposal, where the city council offered to lease a site off Milton Road to Marshall, it was finally agreed in January 1936 that the new aerodrome would be just a little to the east of Fen Ditton at Teversham Corner on land that David Marshall had already bought. From September 1937 Marshall's Flying School was situated at Teversham; Fen Ditton was closed, the hangars demolished, the area compulsorily purchased by the council and later redeveloped for housing. The close proximity of the two sites meant that the aircraft only had to take off, fly over the hedge and land almost immediately.

For the first buildings at the Teversham airfield Arthur Marshall sought advice from Tommy Tomlinson of the University Architectural School and as a result the control building was built in an attractive Art Deco style: distinctive and modern to reflect an industry of the future. Sir Kingsley Wood, Secretary of State for Air, formally opened Marshall's new base on 8 October 1938, an event to which large numbers were invited and entertained to a flying display in which three Spitfires of 19 Squadron, based at Duxford, gave the premiere display of the type. But Teversham had actually been fully functioning since February when the Government had contracted the company to start training pilots. So No.22 Elementary and Reserve Flying School had set to work, equipped with Tiger Moths and Hawker Harts and later two Battles, and by the time the new aerodrome was 'opened' more than 500 pilots had been trained!

At the time of the Munich Crisis in August 1938 further expansion took place with another hangar, lecture halls, a parachute room and accommodation block added. The company co-ordinated all the work so well that they were awarded the accolade of RAF Training Command as the best civil-operated flying training centre in the country. Though these specific facilities were built at government expense as part of the 'shadow factory' strategic dispersal scheme, the initial expansion at Teversham meant that the family had to borrow large sums to finance the purchase of the land and the erection of the buildings. Owning the airfield and buildings gave Marshall independence and security.

Expansion continued, for despite Chamberlain's return from Munich and his 'Peace in our time' rhetoric, people knew that war was imminent and preparations continued in earnest. Night flying was introduced in March 1939 but as this part of the business grew, the motor side entered the doldrums. As was to often prove the case during the company's history its excellent facilities, skilled workforce, sound control and planning meant it was in a good position to react to events and the Air Ministry awarded it the contract for refurbishing and modification of the Armstrong Whitworth Whitley twin-engined bomber. Arthur Marshall and Peter May, one of the Flying School's instructors, collected the first Whitley from RAF Shawbury on Saturday 2 September, the day before Britain declared war on Germany. Arthur moved his office to Teversham and company founder David Marshall came out of retirement to manage the garage in Jesus Lane, which became busy with the manufacture of shell parts and the maintenance of military vehicles just as had been the case in the First World War.

David Marshall, Sir Alan Cobham (who later founded Flight Refuelling) and Arthur Marshall at the opening of the first Marshall aerodrome at Fen Ditton, Cambridge, in June 1929. *(MA)*

A race in progress at the opening of the Fen Ditton aerodrome. Flying in the middle is Dermot Boyle, later Marshal of the Royal Air Force, and on the right Dick Waghorn, who won the Schneider Trophy at Calshot in 1929 flying the Supermarine S.6 at 328.63mph. The current airfield at Teversham is only a few hundred yards to the east of it. The Marshall family home, Whitehill, is to the right of the picture. *(MA)*

Arthur Marshall's first aircraft was G-AAEH, a de Havilland Gipsy Moth, which he bought in 1929 on the beach at Heacham. *(MA)*

In March 1931, Arthur collected a new de Havilland Puss Moth, G-ABIZ, from de Havilland's Stag Lane factory. This was employed on air taxi work and was also used to transport Arthur (as pilot) and his wife on their honeymoon. *(MA)*

Fen Ditton aerodrome in 1931. Parked on the right is Westland Wessex G–ABEG and centrally is Arthur Marshall's Gipsy Moth. With the transfer of the aerodrome to Teversham, this area was redeveloped for housing. *(MA)*

two

The Second World War and its aftermath

During the six years of hostilities the company played a major part in the war effort, repairing, rebuilding or modifying seventeen different types at Teversham. In 1940 the Ministry of Aircraft Production set up the Civil Repair Organisation which directed firms' activities. This work did not only take place on the airfield site but also in the buildings built for commercial vehicle use on the north side of Newmarket Road. If the aircraft arrived by air they were towed across the Newmarket Road, worked on, towed back across the same road, and flight tested on the airfield. To improve security for the many aircraft dispersed about the airfield, Newmarket Road was closed to all civilian traffic for a time.

Though Cambridge remained the centre for activities, Marshall staff were sent all around the country to different sites to carry out local repairs to aircraft. Before the advent of the Whitleys, the initial types worked on were small numbers of biplane fighters, Hawker Harts, Audaxs, Hinds and Gloster Gladiators as well as Fairey Battle monoplanes. Between 1939 and 1944 the company worked on 275 Whitley bombers, 1,100 Airspeed Oxfords and other communications aircraft. Avro Ansons, Hurricanes, Spitfires, Boeing B-17s and Albermarle glider tugs also entered the Marshall hangars in the latter years of the war.

Marshall carried out an extensive programme of work on de Havilland Mosquitoes in 1943-1944. Over one hundred Mosquitoes were fitted with radar noses in 1943 to become Mosquito Mk.12s and in 1944 the company shared work with Vickers-Armstrongs on converting seventeen Mosquitoes to carry 4,000lb bombs. In an even

The new Cambridge aerodrome at Teversham in 1938. *(MA)*

The control building at the new aerodrome side, showing off its Art Deco stylishness. *(MA)*

more 'hush-hush' capacity, Marshall's was involved, along with Vickers and Airspeed, in converting twenty-nine Mosquitoes to carry the Barnes Wallis Highball bouncing bomb. This bomb was a smaller version of the Upkeep bomb used by 617 Squadron's Lancasters in the famous Dambusters raid. The intention was for these Mosquitoes, operated by 617 Squadron, to be aircraft carrier based and to attack major German or Japanese naval targets such as the *Tirpitz*. As it transpired, the end of hostilities meant this bomb was never used in anger.

In the last years of the war there was more conversion and repair work to fill the hangars, with 150 Hawker Typhoons and Dakotas which were to be flown to Cambridge, repaired and rapidly returned to action, to be employed on the D-Day landings and the liberation of France. Other more seriously damaged examples came in by road. Pressure of work became so heavy at this time that for a number of weeks staff were putting in eighty to ninety hours per week each.

The record turnout during the war was thirty-three repairs in a week; made up of eleven rebuilds at Cambridge and twenty-two on site. Marshall's Aircraft Repair Organisation developed to become the largest with a peak employment of 3,200 and more than 5,000 aircraft converted or repaired. These were flight tested by a discreet band of three pilots: Arthur Marshall and Peter May, with Leslie Scratchard joining in 1941. During the war years, Arthur Marshall put in a great many hours test flying aircraft repaired at Teversham, delivering them, and keeping in communication with the various out-stations. Initially he was able to use one of the EFTS Tigers but later used a Miles Falcon, G-ADLI, which had not been requisitioned. At the beginning of the war he had been averaging twelve hours testing per month, by the end this had increased to forty-five hours in addition to all his other duties.

Pilots of the No.22 Elementary and Reserve Flying School in front of a Tiger Moths with the OC, Wing Commander Peter May, on the south aerodrome side of the control building in March 1939. *(MA)*

Aircraft arrived for repair by air and by road but some arrivals were less planned. Battered Westland Lysanders briefly sojourned at Teversham while awaiting a permanent base after the fall of France in summer 1940 and Luftwaffe Dorniers came to bomb them. With invasion apparently imminent Peter May was keen for both Arthur and himself to man armed Gladiators to see off any marauding German aircraft. This deterrent force took to the air three times on August 1940 but never saw action! Later unscheduled arrivals included a Short Stirling bomber which made a forced landing in 1943 and a Boeing B-17 Flying Fortress, with wounded on board, which found refuge on return from a bombing raid over Germany later in the same year.

The Second World War – training 20,000 pilots

With civilian flying banned for the duration of the war, the forty-eight Flying School Tiger Moths became the No.22 Elementary Flying Training School (EFTS) which adopted a seven-day-a-week all-daylight-hours flying policy. The Cambridge University Air Squadron also joined the EFTS. The instructors were enlisted as Sergeant-Pilots and then loaned back to civilian companies, with Peter May as the CO and the rank of Wing Commander. At the beginning of 1940 there were some forty-eight machines in use, which grew to a peak of 126 by the end of hostilities. From 1940 to 1943, a Flying Instructors School was also in operation at Teversham which flew almost 180 aircraft.

With these numbers of aircraft based there, it can be appreciated how busy the Teversham circuit was during these years. Apparently these machines became locally known as 'Marshall's Messerschmitts' at the time. During the war Marshall trained approximately 20,000 pilots at Teversham and its other airfields on Tiger Moths, representing about one in six of all RAF pilots. The Marshall operation was deemed so successful that their model was investigated by the RAF and the company was offered the opportunity to run No.29 EFTS at Clyffe Pypard, near Swindon, which opened with 106 aircraft in 1942 and continued in operation until 1947.

Throughout the war there had been great efforts made by the workers and the Marshall family. David Marshall, who had come out of retirement and had taken on the management the garage and airfield catering at the beginning of the war, died at the age of sixty-nine on 9 July 1942 while riding a horse in Coldhams Lane, which runs just south of the airfield site. Arthur's four elder sisters then ran the airfield canteen until 1947 and so the whole concern very much remained a family business.

Peacetime

The end of the war saw jubilant celebrations in Cambridge with a huge bonfire on Midsummer Common, the flames fuelled by redundant aircraft. But peacetime brought its own challenges. The question for the company now was how could work be found for their 3,000 employees?

The shadow factories, which had produced so many wartime aircraft, were shut down and projects were understandably cancelled, such as Marshall for the fitting of engines to Hamilcar gliders.

Survival is closely linked with the ability to adapt and Marshall, as has been shown before, were quick to respond to the changing marketplace and to peacetime demands. In order to retain their well-trained workers, the vehicle business was resurrected with Airspeed Oxford repair being exchanged for Austin commercial vehicles, a chauffeur-driven service reinstated and a new Peterborough-based motor dealership set up to the north of Cambridge. In no time a contract was negotiated to recommission a wide

Elementary Flying Training School trainee pilots and two Tiger Moths outside a suitably camouflaged hangar. During the war, Marshall's trained approximately 20,000 pilots, which is approximately seventeen per cent of all RAF pilots, at Teversham and its other airfields. *(MA)*

Gloster Gladiators were amongst the types repaired at Cambridge during the war. Three times during August 1940 Peter May, OC of Flying Training, and Arthur Marshall flew armed Gladiators around the area with the intention of attacking any German aircraft. In this photograph they are seen demonstrating during peacetime.
(Derek N. James)

range of military vehicles and to refurbish a large number of London buses, which had received little maintenance during the war.

The company also investigated the opportunities for commercial vehicle body-building which had not been undertaken before and initially had to employ vehicle body specialists before embarking on this new venture. Soon the firm had all the relevant departments set up to engage in manufacture. One of the first customers was Chivers, the fruit growers and jam manufacturers, who were local to Cambridge; Whitbread, the brewers, came next, with a valuable contract derived from Colonel Whitbread's friendship with David Marshall since he had stabled his car at the Jesus Lane garage. Having branched out into commercial vehicles a brand name was a necessity, so in 1948 Marshall Motor Bodies Ltd was established. From then on there were large orders for a great variety of differing vehicle bodies, including 'black marias' and refuse lorries.

On 1 January 1946 civil flying was once more permitted and Lady Bragg, first Lady Mayor of Cambridge, took to the air as the first new student in Tiger Moth G-ACDG. Business grew again surprising quickly, with many anxious to re-acquaint themselves with their flying skills in a peacetime setting and others keen to learn. The airfield was active again so additional aircraft were bought, bringing the Flying School numbers up to six Tiger Moths and two Proctors. De Havilland Rapides were employed on charters which were generally within the UK or Europe but did stray as far as South Africa. The Cambridge No.22 EFTS continued, becoming No.22 Reserve Training School (RTS).

Two types used as training aircraft at Cambridge during the war. In the foreground is a sole North American Harvard and beyond are a number Tiger Moths being tended. *(MA)*

The Airspeed Oxford was the RAF's first twin-engine advanced trainer. Marshall employed Oxfords for flying training and maintained more than 1,200 of type for the RAF during hostilities. *(MA)*

De Havilland Mosquitoes in Hangar 2 during the war. Over one hundred Mosquitoes were fitted with radar in 1943 to become Mosquito Mk.12s, and in 1944 the company shared work with Vickers-Armstrongs on converting seventeen Mosquitoes to carry 4,000lb bombs. *(MA)*

One of the Mosquito Mk.12s converted to a night fighter with radar at Cambridge. *(MA)*

A distinguishing feature of the Marshall wartime work was the equipping of twenty-nine Mosquitoes to carry the Barnes Wallis Highball bomb, a smaller version of the Upkeep used in the Dams raid. Here a Mosquito is seen during a practise drop of an Upkeep. These Mosquitoes would have flown aircraft carrier-based attacks on major naval targets, but in the event the bomb was never used in anger. *(Stephen Flower)*

Between 1939 and 1944 the company carried out maintenance on and repaired 275 Armstrong Whitworth Whitley bombers. The Whitley was one of the mainstays of Bomber Command used as a night bomber in the early part of the war. *(MA)*

Marshall workers posing proudly in front of one of the Armstrong Whitworth Whitley bombers repaired at Cambridge in 1944. *(MA)*

The airfield during the war years. The control building was painted brown and there are many types dispersed around the airfield. These include Oxfords, Tiger Moths and Albermarles. *(MA)*

Avro Anson TX213 at RAF Abingdon in 1968. Ansons were used for communications flying and large numbers were sent to Cambridge for repair during the war. *(Author)*

The Boeing B-17 Fortress joined the list of aircraft repaired by Marshall during the war when one arrived in March 1943. This example, 124485 *Sally B*, is based at the Imperial War Museum, Duxford. *(Author)*

The ninety-strong Marshall Fire Section posed in 1944 outside the control building which was painted brown during the war years. *(Cambridgeshire Libraries)*

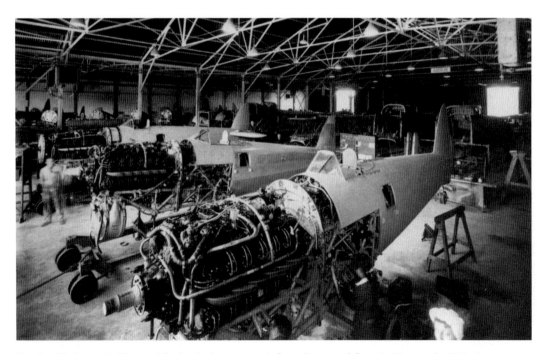

Hawker Typhoons in Hangar 6 for battle damage repair from the second front in Normandy 1944. In the background are Armstrong Whitworth Albemarle fuselages. The Albemarles were used as Glider tugs in Africa and at the Normandy landings. *(Bedford Lemere & Co.)*

Many Dakotas were repaired at Teversham, especially after D-Day. This example, though in the D-Day colour scheme, is actually South African registered and was hangared at Teversham in the 1980s. Dakotas also came for repair during the Berlin airlift in 1948. *(MA)*

Outside the still-camouflaged control building on 1 January 1946, Lady Bragg, Mayor of Cambridge, took to the air as the first new student in Tiger Moth G-ACDG. On the right is Marshall's-owned Miles Falcon G-ADLI. Left to right are: Arthur Marshall, Lady Bragg, Norman De Bruyne, Leslie Worsdell (Marshall's test pilot), Douglas Winton-Smith. *(Cambridge Daily News)*

Demonstration of the prototype de Havilland Dove G-AGPJ at Cambridge on 11 August 1946. *(MA)*

Marshall converted the first RAF Spitfire to civilian use as G-AHZI and it was named *Josephine* in October 1946 for M.L. Bramson. It crashed on take-off from Kastrup, Copenhagen, on 15 April 1947. *(Cambridgeshire Libraries)*

Line-up of Marshall's types in 1947: Percival Proctor, Miles Falcon, G–ADLI (which Arthur Marshall used throughout the war), two Tiger Moths. *(Cambridgeshire Libraries)*

Marshall vehicles on show at Earls Court in 1948. In the aftermath of war the company sought diversification, so commercial vehicle manufacture began. An important local customer for vehicles was Whitbread who ordered drays. *(MA)*

'Black Maria'! A Metropolitan Police prison van, built in 1948. *(MA)*

Above: The Marshall Jesus Lane car showrooms with an Austin Princess on display. The board on the right advertises 'Driving tuition, Flying tuition, Air Charter'.

Left: Austin House, Marshall's car showrooms in Jesus Lane. It was the site of the main office from 1912 to 1939 and continued in use as a garage until 2000. *(Both courtesy of Cambridgeshire Libraries)*

three

The Cold War Years

Refurbishment of de Havilland Vampires taking place in hangars at Waterbeach, just three miles north of the Marshall base at Teversham. It was convenient to use Waterbeach because it possessed a hard runway. (MA)

The de Havilland connection

After the challenge of the early post-war years, military re-equipping began at the factory place alongside civil aviation interests. Marshall had sensibly maintained good relations with the major manufacturers, especially de Havilland for whom the company continued to work on Mosquitoes and Hornets after 1945, fitting ninety-nine of the former with radar. Hatfield-based de Havilland had entered the jet age with their Vampire 1943 which was also powered by a de Havilland Goblin jet engine. But with the pressure of other development work in early 1950 de Havilland passed over to Marshall all the work on Vampires for repair, refurbishment, modification or preparation to customer specification, thus allowing them to concentrate on future developments.

Marshall were normally only engaged in working on the finished product but in 1953 de Havilland was so over-worked that Marshall was employed to assemble the final eighty-four Venoms, a Ghost-powered development of the Vampire. The wartime manner of operation was resumed. The hangars on the north side of Newmarket Road were once more put to aircraft use for the final assembly of the machines which arrived in kit form from de Havilland. On completion, traffic on Newmarket Road was stopped and they were towed across the road to the airfield. Further work on the small de Havilland jets continued when the company was rewarded with a 2½ year contract from de Havilland to fit 284 Vampires T.11 trainers with ejector seats.

The firm realised that to continue to obtain work they would need to improve their facilities by building a tarmac runway, so land to the south of the airfield was bought to provide room for a runway. Construction of a narrow concrete runway only 80ft wide and 4,465ft long started in 1953 and was completed in the following year. While runway construction was taking place, a hangar was rented at nearby Waterbeach as a flight test base for the Venoms

Though Marshall were normally only engaged in working on finished aircraft, in 1953 de Havilland was so overworked that Marshall's assembled the final eighty-four Venoms to be built, using the hangars on the north side of Newmarket Road. The finished aircraft were then wheeled across to the aerodrome on the south side to be flown. *(MA)*

The work on de Havilland jets continued when in 1954 the company was rewarded with a 2½ year contract to fit 284 Vampires T.11 trainers with ejector seats. WZ590 pictured here is now at the Imperial War Museum, Duxford. *(MA)*

Comet 2R XK659 taking off at Luqa, Malta, in 1971. It was originally destined for service with BOAC and registered as G-AMXC, but after the Comet accidents and because of their high performance, three Comet 2s were reconfigured for service as Electronic Reconnaissance aircraft with the RAF by Marshall. Redesignated as a Comet 2R, XK659 flew with the RAF until 8 April 1974 when the new Nimrod R.1s replaced it. *(MAP)*

Hush-hush Comets

With all the work that the company had already carried out on their Mosquitoes, Hornets, Vampires and Venoms, Marshall had established a firm connection with de Havilland's and were called upon to convert several Comet 2s to a special military specification in 1955. These aircraft had all been built as part of BOAC's order for Comet 2s but with the disasters that befell the Comet 1 all orders were cancelled, leaving de Havilland in dire straits. Fortunately the Ministry of Supply purchased a large number of the Comet 2s for RAF use. Some, which were still being built, were heavily modified with strengthened skins so that they could safely take full cabin pressurisation but three already completed were allocated to Marshall's. These aircraft – originally registered as G-AMXA, 'MXC, 'MXE – were delivered to Cambridge in 1955 for conversion, to become electronic surveillance aircraft. They were delivered in 1957–1958 initially to 192 Squadron (which later became 51 Squadron) as XK655, XK659, XK663 respectively. In 1959 XK663 was burned in a hangar fire at Wyton, so a further Comet 2, XK695, was taken off normal RAF transport duties and sent to Cambridge for conversion to 2R status in 1961 and delivered two years later. These aircraft continued in use until 1974; XK695 was preserved at Duxford but was unfortunately scrapped in 1992.

Although the de Havilland contract was valuable, Arthur Marshall was aware of the danger of being reliant on a small number of customers. He sought meetings with the managers of Bristol, English Electric and Vickers, and visited each in turn giving them a thorough presentation of the full service that his company could offer: from minor repair through to final assembly, and flight test to manufacturers' specification.

Marshall and Vickers

Arthur Marshall's prescience was rewarded shortly afterwards when Vickers offered work on their three twin-engined transports: the Viking airliner and its two military versions, the Valetta and Varsity. Initially Marshall worked on modifications for sixty-one Varsities and continued with various other activities such as modifications or servicing on the type until 1969. The firm also worked on its older sister, the Valetta, carrying out conversion work between 1956 and 1963. As the work with Vickers began, Bristol also offered the firm a contract to fit radar to twenty-three Brigands light bombers.

Viscounts at Cambridge

By 1954 Vickers were under a lot of pressure, working simultaneously on the Viscount, Valiant and several other projects, and had no spare hangar capacity. In the winter of 1954/55 Marshall were thus called upon to help with a modification programme to BEA's Viscount 701s. (One of these, G-ALWF, the second production aircraft, is preserved at Imperial War Museum at Duxford some fifteen miles south of Cambridge.) Marshall were able to shoehorn five Viscounts into one of their hangars; though as it was unheated working conditions must have left much to be desired.

On 13 December 1954 BEA Viscount 701 G-AMOB was involved in an abandoned take-off while crew-training at Blackbushe and ran off the runway, collapsing the undercarriage. Though seriously damaged it was dismantled and dispatched by road to Cambridge for repair. Just over a month later, on 16 January, Viscount G-AMOK took off on the stub of a disused runway at Heathrow in poor visibility and collided with a steel barrier. It was similarly transported to Marshall's for rebuild. Appreciating that there was much more Viscount work to come and that one of the critical success factors was hangar capacity, the firm built more hangars which were soon full of aircraft.

A more serious event took place on 14 March 1957 when the first production Viscount, G-ALWE the flagship of BEA's fleet, was on approach to Manchester when it went into an uncontrollable bank and crashed into houses at Wythenshawe. The cause was metal fatigue leading to flap failure and aileron lock. All BEA's Viscounts were withdrawn from service while investigations took place. After the identification of the accident's cause all the Viscounts had to be modified, some being sent to Vickers for repair but the bulk went to Cambridge where the test pilots had to learn how to carry out flapless landings on the Teversham runway. Fortunately the runway had been extended and widened earlier in the year and was now 5,220ft long and conformed to the standard width of 150ft. Marshall's later continued to work on the BEA Viscounts, reconfiguring them to two crew operation by removing the radio operators' position and regularly providing crew for Trans-Canada Airlines Viscount delivery flights which went via Scotland, Iceland and Greenland. In later years other Viscount work included Iraqi Airways' YI-ACL, rebuilt after a heavy landing at Mosul in Iraq, and a Pakistani Air Force machine received an executive interior. Some of BEA's early Viscounts returned, now quite at home at Cambridge, for storage or reworking for new owners such as Cambrian Airways.

Marshall worked on modifications for sixty-one Vickers Varsities and continued with various activities on the type, including autoland work at RAE Bedford and servicing until 1969. *(Author)*

The firm also worked on the elder sister of the Varsity, the Vickers Valetta, converting Valetta T.3s to T.4s by fitting radar and a specially elongated nose to help train Javelin pilots. VW162, a C Mk.1, is shown here at Cambridge in 1964. *(NA3T/ATPH photograph)*

As Vickers had no spare hangar capacity, Marshall were called on to help with a modification programme to BEA's Viscount 701s in the winter of 1954/55. One of these, G-MOA, is seen here at Cambridge. *(NA3T/ATPH photograph)*

The Valiant years

The Vickers Valiant first flew in 1951 and, with the Handley Page Victor and Avro Vulcan, was the first of a trio of V bombers. Between 1951 and 1957 a total of 107 were built and virtually all of these visited Teversham at some time in their short lives for major or minor work. The aircraft provided the company with a great amount of work between 1956 and 1964, but when severe cracks were found in their rear spars it was decided that it was uneconomic to repair them and the entire fleet was grounded in December 1964.

During 1955 the company did an appreciable amount of the design work on the Valiant, which naturally stood them in good stead when Vickers were short of capacity and needed help with modification work. Since Arthur Marshall had had the good sense to provide more hangar capacity, his firm was ready to take on more work.

The first Valiant WZ368 arrived at Cambridge on 30 January 1956 and at a time when the runway was only 80ft wide and 4,465ft long. Soon Vickers Chief Test Pilot, Jock Bryce, made the point that their aircraft could not safely be operated from this runway, colloquially known as 'the bootlace'. Unwilling to halt Valiant work while the runway was widened, Marshall were able to get agreement from the Ministry that they could continue test flying on the runway even while work was in progress. It was an amazing decision in the light of today's stringent safety regulations since during take-off or landing a Valiant's right wing would only be ten feet clear of the concreting equipment while the left undercarriage leg was only two foot clear of the grass!

The Valiant was the first British aircraft to drop a free-fall nuclear weapon, which took place in 1956. Then in the late 1950s with the intensification of the Cold War, the Avro Blue Steel nuclear missile was developed. This was 25ft long and capable of Mach 2.5 at an altitude of 75,000ft. (In contemporary terms this would be deemed a

BEA's Viscount G-AMOB in a sorry state after running off the runway at Blackbushe after an abandoned take-off on 13 December 1954. Normally such serious damage would have resulted in a write-off but, as Viscounts were in such short supply, Marshall's were called in and carried out a complete rebuild, delivering it back to BEA in May 1956. *(Cambridgeshire Libraries)*

Four Vickers Valiants at Cambridge. Marshall carried out design, servicing and many major modifications on virtually the entire Valiant bomber fleet between 1956 and 1964. XD816, in the foreground, was the last Valiant flying and its nose survives at the Brooklands Museum in Surrey. *(MA)*

cruise missile.) Valiant WZ375 was used as a test vehicle and initially flew with a forty-per-cent scale model of Blue Steel after conversion by Marshall in 1957. But then a requirement was developed for tests of full-scale examples so the company assisted Vickers-Armstrongs by converting three other machines – WP204 and WZ373 and the original WZ375 – to carry full-scale Blue Steel rounds in 1958-1959. This entailed removing the navigator's and flight engineer's stations, the installation of an Inertial Navigation System and specially engineered beams in the aircraft's bomb bay. Though the Valiant never went on to carry the missile in active service, it proved important in the development and later active service installation in the Vulcan and Victor. Such was the high regard that Vickers and the RAF held for the Marshall that it granted the company design authority for the Valiant's electrical systems.

In April 1962, at height of the Cold War, the RAF wanted their Deterrent Force airborne in four minutes to preclude Russian attack. To achieve this stern challenge, Marshall's pilots and engineers created a scheme for the pitot heads to be automatically uncovered and all four engines simultaneously started enabling a take-off within the target time. They demonstrated this to Bomber Group but the AOC (Air Officer Commanding) was alarmed by risk of the pitots being uncovered in this manner and banned further use. But some elements of the Marshall procedure were incorporated in the scheme to get the V bombers airborne in four minutes.

The Canberra

The firm became involved with the English Electric Canberra five years after its maiden flight in 1949 when the first machines arrived for modification and development work. In fact the company was entrusted with all modification and development work on in-service machines. A good example of the company's work on the type is WT333, built as a B(I)8 in 1956 and delivered straight from the manufacturers to Cambridge. This was virtually gutted to fit the Low Altitude Bombing System (LABS) necessary for nuclear bomb trials and continued on in experimental use, overhauled at Marshall's in 1964 and until ultimately preserved at Bruntingthorpe in Lincolnshire. Later, specialised modification kits were manufactured at Cambridge to convert Canberra B6s to B15 and B16 standard. This involved updating avionics and installation of LABS to carry a 2,000lb nuclear bomb. In the early 1970s Marshall's bought second-hand models for refurbishment and, with BAC's, support received an order from Peru for eleven aircraft in 1973. Similar work continued on Canberras until 1978.

While the company was profitably involved in all military work, there were also lesser but still important other moneymaking activities. For example all eighteen of BOAC's Britannias 312s passed briefly through Teversham in 1957-1958, being prepared to final delivery standard for their owner. Meanwhile several Airspeed Ambassadors were fitted with freight doors to enable them to transport horses.

Not all of the work undertaken necessarily took place at Cambridge; occasionally it happened at the contractor's, so Marshall sent teams to carry out work elsewhere. A major feature of the firm was the strength of its design office which manufacturers called upon to help them out as necessary. Just as Vickers had sub-contracted out Valiant design work to Marshall's, they also called on their assistance with the design of the Vickers V1000 airliner. Saunders-Roe used their designers for their ill-fated Saro SR 177 jet/rocket fighter and so did Bristol for the 188 supersonic research jet. Another customer for this service was English Electric, which used Marshall's design services for some of its Lightning F3 work.

No.7 Squadron's Valiant B1 XD830 parked on the Cambridge apron in 1958. *(NA3T/ATPH photograph)*

At Teversham in the 1950s, one of the many Canberra B2s worked on by the firm. This example, WD962, made a record flight from London to Tripoli in 2 hours 41 minutes, at an average speed of 538mph, on 18 February 1952. Nine years later it was scrapped at Farnborough. *(NA3T/ATPH photograph)*

WH967, an English Electric Canberra B6 built by Shorts which was converted to a B15 at Cambridge. English Electric contracted Marshall to introduce new armaments and avionics with provision for LABS (Low Altitude Bombing System). After producing a prototype conversion, which first flew on 4 October 1960, the company then produced a total of seventy-four conversions. *(MA)*

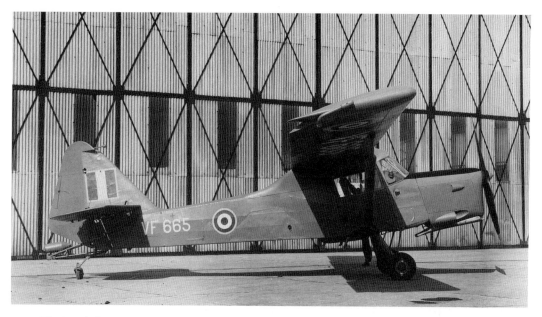

The Marshall MA4, VF665, an Auster T.7 heavily modified for boundary layer control and low drag research. It was fitted with a new porous, high-aspect ratio wing, larger all-flying tail and stronger landing gear. Ailerons could be drooped and spoilers were fitted. Suction for the wing was provided by a small gas turbine in the rear fuselage. Visible in this photograph are the spin recovery parachute and heavily wool-tufted wings. It first flew in 1959 but crashed in 1966, killing its crew of two. *(MA)*

Marshall's MA4

Marshall's have never built an aircraft from new though they have carried out massive modifications and rebuilds of countless types. Notwithstanding there was one aircraft that actually bears the company's name. It was the Marshall MA4, a version of an Auster built for boundary layer control and low drag research funded by the Ministry of Aviation and operated by Cambridge University Engineering Department. So a new Auster T.7 VF665 was sent straight from the production line at Rearsby, Leicestershire, to Teversham. Retaining its engine, it was fitted with a new porous high-aspect ratio wing, larger all-flying tail and stronger landing gear. Ailerons could be drooped and spoilers were fitted. Suction for the wing was provided by a small gas turbine in the rear fuselage. A spin recovery parachute was also fitted. Designated as the Marshall MA4, it did not fly until early 1959 though this was not made public knowledge until late 1960. Much of the flying was done at near stalling speed and the MA4 could be flown down to 39 knots though with an angle of incidence of 45 degrees. The test programme continued until 1966 when the aircraft flown by Brian Wass, one of Marshall test pilots, crashed near Linton, Cambridgeshire, killing him and the flight test observer, Krishnamirthy. Last seen in an inverted spin the cause of the accident to the Marshall MA4 was never explained and remains a mystery.

Throughout the 1950s work also continued on the ever important vehicle side. A good example of the Marshall way – ever ready to rise to a challenge and meet expectations – was the award of a major contract from the Ministry of Supply for

BOAC Bristol Britannia 312s – G-AOVC, 'D and 'M – in the Cambridge hangars for fitting out in late May 1958. All of the airline's Britannia 312s passed through Teversham for modification to final delivery standard. *(MA)*

Exotic Cubana Britannia at Cambridge in 1961. In the background is Valiant WP209. *(MA)*

3,027 all-metal three-ton cargo bodies which had all to be delivered within twelve months. Production reached a peak of 120 of these per week. These were not the only challenging vehicle orders received: 18,833 bodies were fabricated between 1950 and 1957.

Another characteristic of the Marshall way was their alacrity to seize a new opportunity. At the end of the 1950s Arthur Marshall quickly took advantage of the offer of purchasing Mulliners' bus division. This gave the firm the opportunity to buy a going concern and during the 1960s the firm built 1,200 single and double-deckers for home and overseas, exporting to more than thirty countries.

Marshall in the 1960s

At the beginning of the decade there was a major reorganisation of the British aircraft industry at the behest of the Conservative Government. Vickers-Armstrongs, English Electric and Bristol merged to form the British Aircraft Corporation (BAC) while Armstrong Whitworth, Avro, Blackburn de Havilland and Hawker joined together as Hawker Siddeley Aviation (HSA). Handley Page refused to join the others but only lasted the decade as an independent force.

As the sixties dawned, the company was as busy as ever with both large and small projects: from maintaining Chipmunks for the UCAS (University of Cambridge Air Squadron) to maintaining all the various training aircraft at RAF Shawbury which it managed from 1961 to 1991.

In 1959 Skyways' Lockheed Constellation G-ARXE visited for avionics installation. Note the Lufthansa Viscount in the background. *(MA)*

Gulfstream

In 1960 the company was appointed Service Centre for all models of Gulfstream by the manufacturer for the complete outfitting of their aircraft, often in 'green' condition. This type of project was carried through from inception, when initial requirements were discussed with the customer, through to design and installation stages of fittings and avionics, to final flight test and acceptance. As an example, in 1964 the firm fitted out a Gulfstream for King Constantine of Greece. Just as Marshall often repaired Viscounts they also undertook major repairs on Gulfstreams damaged in service, including on-site temporary repairs to permit flight to Cambridge, to be followed by full repair.

Even though the structure of the aircraft industry was changing with the formation of much larger groupings, Vickers (now part of the British Aircraft Corporation) called on the company's help again in 1961-1962 to modify seven Vanguards which had already briefly entered service with BEA. In 1964 they again called on the firm to refurbish three VC10s which had been part of the flight test programme and now had to be brought up to delivery standard for BOAC. This contract amounted to 150,000 man-hours per aircraft.

The end of Canberra and Valiant work

After the success of their work on the English Electric Canberra, Marshall was engaged by them to the design the electrical installation of the supersonic Lightning fighter. And for English Electric's parent BAC, there were more than 400,000 man-hours of design work on the TSR2, which unfortunately came to an end with the project's cancellation in April 1965.

As a result of the demise of the Valiant (see above) and the cancellation of the BAC TSR2, the firm was to experience a sudden shortfall in work. This was exacerbated by BAC (English Electric) calling in all their Canberra work to provide their own workers with employment. As these major continuing projects evaporated the organisation had to make do with older contracts. However, the shrewdness shown by the family in not only specialising in aviation but also in motor vehicle work meant that work could be found for the Marshall employees in vehicle body construction. Under Michael Marshall's leadership the vehicle business has expanded by takeovers of various dealerships in the East Anglian region.

Work may have been reduced but it did not dry up completely. There was always other work such as executive fitting out of BAC One-Elevens, the first example being BAC's demonstrator G-ASYE in preparation for its World Tours in 1966. And two years later another One-Eleven customer, the Brazilian Air Force, needed a special avionics fit and long-range tanks in their two machines.

Marshall Aerospace even had a hand in designing the wing for the USAF'S Lockheed C5A Galaxy, a massive military transport aircraft. They designed and built a full-scale mock-up of the mainplane and surfaces for Lockheed's London design office which was set up by the American manufacturer after the loss of jobs caused by the Labour Government's decision to cancel a number of major aircraft projects in 1964-1965. The mock-up was transported to Lockheed's plant at Marietta, Georgia, in 1967. This work may well have helped in cementing the Hercules deal which has now been a major source of income for almost forty years.

Iraqi Airways Vickers Viscount YI-ACL came to Cambridge in 1958 after a heavy landing at Mosul, Iraq, which tore off the undercarriage. Two years later it was redelivered to Iraqi Airways. *(MA)*

A further Viscount visitor was XR802, which after airline use arrived at Cambridge for conversion for the Empire Test Pilots School in January 1962. *(Author)*

Marshall was first involved with the de Havilland Canada Chipmunk in 1960, maintaining them for the Cambridge University Air Squadron and at RAF Shawbury until 1999. *(MA)*

Under contract to RAE Farnborough, the third production Avro Shackleton Mk.3, WR972, was fitted in 1961 with a special rear fuselage blunt faring for experimentation with anti-spin and braking parachutes. *(MAP)*

Airspeed Ambassador G-ALZR. After service with BEA, she became Tyne testbed with Rolls-Royce, and then in 1964 was fitted of a freight door by Marshall and delivered to BKS Air Transport Cargo Division. *(NA3T/ATPH photograph)*

After the war a fleet of four Dragon Rapides were used for air charter work providing a handy source of income. However, in 1962 the last one, G-AGZO, was sold to France. *(MA)*

Above: During the 1950s the company continued with its vehicle work and took on large contract to refurbish military trucks. It has been a regular supplier to the British Army and overseas forces ever since. *(MA)*

Right: In January 1959 the firm delivered its 10,000th cargo vehicle to the Ministry of Supply. *(MA)*

There were other clients for vehicle bodies, such as West Ham for whom this refuse lorry body was built on a Commer chassis in 1960. *(MA)*

Bus bodies were a significant source of income for the firm after the war until 2002. Many were sold in the UK and for export. *(MA)*

Many types have been stored at Teversham. Between 1962 and 1965 most of BOAC's Britannia fleet of 102 was parked there. Six are visible in this picture, along with two Valiants, a Valetta and several light aircraft. *(MA)*

Originally a USAAF Douglas C-47 with the registration 43-48804, this machine was given to Montgomery for his personal use by Eisenhower. It served as KN628 in the RAF until 1955 when it was bought by Derby Aviation as G-AOGZ and is seen visiting Cambridge in 1964. *(NA3T/ATPH photograph)*

Various manufacturers called on the firm's design services after the war, including Bristol for assistance in the design of the high-speed research Bristol 188. Two were produced and the second of these, XF926, is preserved at the RAF Museum Cosford. *(Author)*

Another customer for design services was English Electric, which used Marshall's design services for some of its Lightning work. Pictured here is Lightning F.6 XS931. *(Author)*

Though the BAC TSR2 was cancelled in 1965, it is generally held that it would have been great success. BAC contracted much design work and some manufacture, including the flight-refuelling probe to the company. Two TSR2s are preserved and the fourth production aircraft, XR222, which never flew is at the Imperial War Museum at Duxford. *(Author)*

In 1964 BAC contracted the firm to refurbish three Vickers VC10s after use in the test programme to bring them up to delivery standard. The total work involved 150,000 man-hours. G-ARVE, the fifth production Standard VC10, is shown in the Cambridge hangars. *(MA)*

Pictured here is Viscount 839 EP-MRS undergoing executive conversion for the Royal Australian Air Force in 1964. *(NA3T/ATPH photograph)*

Visit of the Duke of Edinburgh to Cambridge in July 1964 with Michael and Sir Arthur Marshall on his right. *(MA)*

Lockheed's employed the company to design and build a full-scale mock-up of the mainplane and surfaces for the huge Galaxy military transport destined for the USAF. The mock-up was transported to Lockheed's plant at Marietta, Georgia, in 1967. *(MA)*

A USAF Lockheed C-5 Galaxy showing its 222ft wingspan, for which Marshall designed the wing mock-up. *(MA)*

Marshall's fitted executive interiors to many One-Elevens, including BAC's demonstrator, G-ASYE, which is seen here at Gatwick in October 1965. *(BAE SYSTEMS)*

Brazilian Air Force BAC One-Eleven VC92-2110 was fitted with additional fuel tanks, long-range avionics and an executive interior. *(Author)*

After their experience with the Brazilian Air Force One-Elevens, Marshall assisted Hawker Siddeley with the avionics for the HS 125s ordered for the Brazilian Air Force. VC93-2125 is seen at Hatfield in 1969. *(Author)*

Avro Anson 2, G-AGPG, visiting Cambridge in 1968. She had flown for many years as a 'hack' for her makers before being sold to Ekco as a radar demonstrator in 1967, which used her for two years. *(NA3T/ATPH photograph)*

Between 1969 and 1975 the company painted 130 Isle of Wight-built Britten-Norman Islanders. *(Author)*

A Marshall nose for Concorde

From that early relationship with Vickers more work was still to flow. The initial Concorde prototypes were designed and flown with a droop nose, which in the raised position was fitted with a metal visor and which, in the event of failure, would totally obscure vision. The pilots were adamant that this was impossible and a total redesign was demanded. BAC then called on Arthur Marshall to see if his company could redesign it, which the firm accepted with alacrity. So they were responsible for the design, manufacture, test and final assembly up to production standard for the variable geometry nose. This was not their only Concorde work since they also designed most of the flight deck installation.

Indicative of the confidence felt in the firm was the manner in which BAC asked them at short notice to redesign the Concorde's droop nose after it had been decided that the solution used for the initial prototypes would be impossible for airline service. Here is the cockpit and droop nose engineering mock-up in subsonic flight position. *(MA)*

Here is the Concorde mock-up with its nose cone in a raised position for supersonic flight. *(MA)*

The real thing in landing configuration – Marshall leading the way with Concorde!

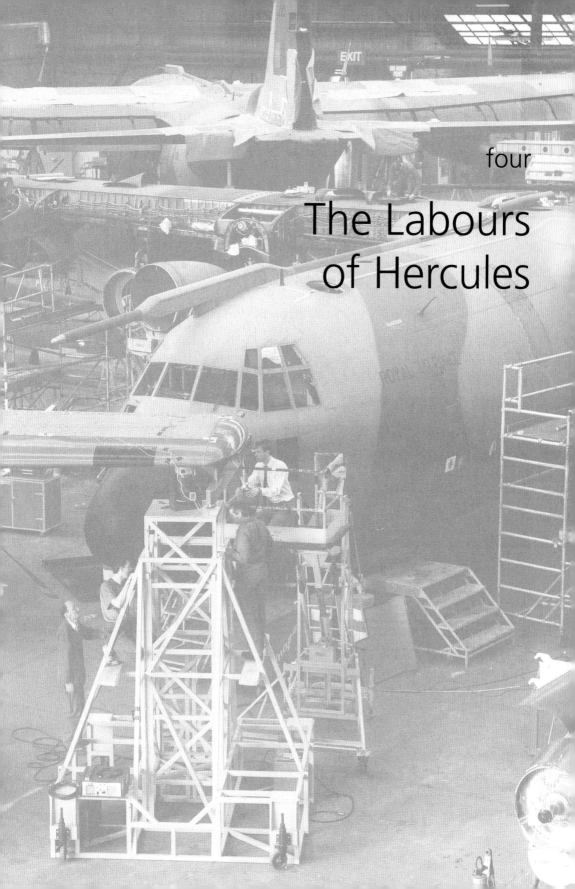

four

The Labours
of Hercules

On 19 December 1966, XV177 the first Lockheed C-130K for the RAF arrived at Cambridge, having flown directly from the USA. The reason for this arrival was the appointment of Marshall as the UK's technical centre for the sixty-six Hercules aircraft purchased for the RAF. This major contract was again due to the perspicacity of Arthur Marshall. In 1964 the Labour Government had cancelled the HS681, a STOL jet transport, leaving the air force with an unfulfilled requirement for a transport aircraft. As negotiations between the Government and Lockheed continued, Marshall proposed themselves as the first Lockheed-appointed Service Centre to the American manufacturer. Lockheed were initially unenthusiastic, wanting to deal directly with the RAF. What was being offered to Lockheed was the service that Marshall had offered to Vickers, English Electric and Bristol over the years. Eventually Lockheed was won round and the Hercules contract started with the arrival at Cambridge of the first RAF aircraft for painting, autopilot fit and production test flying.

On winning this contract the firm then set about training its engineers and pilots in all aspects of their new charge. Only a few years after delivery of the fleet the aircraft were struck down by a major corrosion problem and so the firm had to manage an extensive programme of repairs of varying extent depending upon how badly each aircraft was affected. The company had to replace some wing centre sections and then completely rebuild the outer wings. The problem was so severe that in March 1970 there were seventeen Hercules at Cambridge because of tank corrosion. More work was carried out on the wings from 1975 when the wings were all rebuilt to the latest Lockheed specification.

XV208 was withdrawn from its normal service role to become a meteorological research machine. It returned to Teversham and was fitted with a large nose probe, and its weather radar was then moved above its nose. Not surprisingly it has been nicknamed 'Snoopy'. (MA)

Snoopy

In November 1967, XV208 was delivered to the RAF as a standard specification C Mk.1, but after several years it was sent back to Cambridge in 1972 for conversion to a very 'one-off' state. In the following year it emerged from the Marshall hangars as the one and only Hercules W Mk.2 for the Meteorological Research Flight, with a huge 16ft long air sampling nose probe and the displaced radar mounted in a pod above the nose. Air sampling equipment was fitted along with sophisticated avionics. The scientific staff on board were accommodated in a mobile laboratory sited within the fuselage. Snoopy was delivered in 1973 and remained in service until March 2001, and is currently stored at Boscombe Down.

Stretching Hercules

In the late 1970s the RAF decided to take advantage of the Hercules performance to stretch some of the fleet. One aircraft, XV223 acting as prototype, was converted by Lockheed at Marietta with Marshall's staff in attendance. Then twenty-nine more airframes were converted at Cambridge. The modification consisted of trisecting the fuselage and inserting two plugs into the fuselage, one of 80ins and the other of 100ins. These plugs increased the length of the aircraft by 15ft and the volumetric capacity by thirty-seven per cent, or 1,200cu.ft. All machines were rewired, repainted and flight tested. They were redesignated as Hercules C Mk.3.

Stretching the Hercules! In 1978 the Ministry of Defence decided to lengthen thirty of the C-130 fleet. The first aircraft was engineered at Lockheed's plant at Marietta, Georgia, but the remaining twenty-nine were stretched at Cambridge. Designated as Hercules C Mk.3, it has thirty-seven per cent greater fuselage volume. *(MA)*

The Hercules and Operation Corporate

During the Falklands conflict in 1982, code-named Operation Corporate, it was necessary to extend the Hercules' range when flying from the UK to the British staging post in the mid-Atlantic, Ascension Island, and on to the Falkland Islands. The Ministry of Defence thus asked the company to design and fit flight-refuelling equipment to a number of Hercules, which were thereby able to perform these additional operational tasks.

Instructed to proceed on 15 April 1982 by working flat out, the prototype XV200 was modified to take a flight-refuelling probe by April 25 and was ready to proceed to the Falkland Islands on 5 May 1982. Just twenty-one days from the request being made. Eventually all the RAF's Hercules received a flight-refuelling probe at Cambridge.

A much greater job was the installation of a Hose Drum Unit on the rear door of the aircraft to make it a flight refueller, not just a receiver. The first aircraft, XV296, flew in on 1 May 1982 and was delivered to Boscombe Down for acceptance tests on 11 June. These tests continued apace and the Hercules C Mk.1 (K) was delivered to RAF Lyneham for squadron service on 19 July. Design, manufacture, ground and flight testing was completed on four machines in eighty-seven days. Subsequently two further Hercules were modified in this manner.

Most recently Marshall has begun a programme of cockpit upgrades on the C-130. The upgrade included standardisation modifications, structural refurbishment and miscellaneous repairs. The upgrade incorporates several new mission-enhancing systems, including a flight management system (FMS), automatic flight control system (AFCS), navigation, radio navigation, electronic warfare (EW) self-protection, intercom and flight deck.

The company Hercules Service Centre has given support to over seventy operators worldwide and has dealt with thousands of requirements for servicing and modification work.

Working flat out the prototype XV200 was modified to take a flight-refuelling probe by 25 April and was ready to proceed to the Falkland Islands on 5 May 1982: just twenty-one days from the request being made. *(MA)*

Right: The next challenge was to fit a Hose Drum Unit (HDU) to transfer fuel to other aircraft. The unit was installed on the Hercules rear cargo door on a special frame. In the photograph, the door pivot from the hinges at the bottom right and the HDU will deploy the hose out from the left. *(MA)*

Above: First aircraft flew in on 1 May 1982 and was delivered to Boscombe Down for acceptance tests on 11 June. These tests continued apace and the Hercules C Mk.1 (K) was delivered to RAF Lyneham for squadron service on 19 July. Design, manufacture, ground and flight testing was completed on four machines in eighty-seven days. This is what it looks like from the tanker's perspective. *(MA)*

Right: ... And this is from the receiving end. *(MA)*

RAF Hercules airborne from Cambridge. *(MA)*

Replacing the RAF's Hercules

Replacing the RAF's workhorse is very difficult so there has been an ongoing upgrade programme to keep in the air twenty-five of the original Lockheed C-130K Hercules bought in 1967. It is intended that these aircraft remain operational until the British Government selects and receives their replacement. A major overhaul and avionics programme, undertaken by Marshall Aerospace to ensure that the RAF's 'long-term' Hercules, will remain fully operational until the target out-of-service date in 2007-2008.

As part of the programme to maintain the RAF's Hercules fleet a new hangar, finished in June 2003, will house the rig to fatigue-test the fuselage of a RAF C-130K Hercules aircraft. The tests will simulate the normal service operations of the fuselage, including the application of internal pressure (to simulate cabin pressurisation) combined with external mechanical loading (using hydraulic actuators) to simulate both ground and in-flight loading conditions. The data collected from the testing will be fed back into the maintenance programmes of the RAF C-130K fleet to ensure continued structural integrity in service.

The new C-130J

Meanwhile the oldest of the original twenty-five RAF Hercules fleet have now been replaced by twenty-five new Lockheed Martin C-130J Hercules transport aircraft; delivery of which began on 23 November 1999.

The first customer for the Lockheed C-130J Hercules, effectively a major revamp of the aircraft's design and systems, was the RAF, which had ordered the twenty-five in December 1994. Of these, fifteen are stretched C-130J-30, designated C Mk.4, with the final ten as standard C-130Js, designated Hercules C Mk.5. Five additional aircraft are subject to option and the total value of contract is just over £1 billion. Marshall is acting as Lockheed Martin's UK partner, much as it had with the earlier C-130K.

As part of the C-130J programme on 19 March 1994, a fifty-hour 'single engine demonstrator' flight programme began to test the propulsion system installation characteristics and measure propeller/shaft stress, noise and vibration with the Allison AE 2100 engine and Dowty Aerospace R391 propeller. RAF Hercules C Mk.1 XV181 was the test vehicle, with the trial engine mounted on the inner port position by Marshall Aerospace of Cambridge.

The initial RAF aircraft C-130J-30, a Hercules C Mk.4 ZH865, was formally rolled out at Marietta, Georgia, on 18 October 1995. Owing to the rather troublesome test programme, the initial British delivery was not until August 1998; ZH865 arrived at Boscombe Down on 26 August for the start of clearance trials.

A further eleven aircraft were flown into UK by the end of 1998 for temporary storage and final preparation for delivery to RAF by Marshall Aerospace. One of these, ZH873, was exhibited at the Farnborough Air Show in early September 1998 but the first in-service deliveries were not until November 1999. By the end of that year a total of twenty-two had arrived in UK, with the number delivered to RAF by mid-April 2000 having risen to seven. The remaining eighteen of the original order were delivered by June the following year.

Meanwhile, with over seventy countries operating the C-130 Hercules in its many variants, the upgrade market for these aircraft is currently buoyant. Marshall Aerospace is Lockheed Martin's UK partner for Hercules support and has upgraded South Africa's fleet of ten C-130B/F Hercules and recently sold three refurbished ex-RAF models to the Austrian Air Force.

This original contact between Sir Arthur and Lockheed's which resulted in the Hercules deal has paid and will continue to pay massive dividends to the company. The city of Cambridge is also a beneficiary since at any one time twenty per cent of the RAF's Hercules fleet is at Teversham.

A scene that has now been commonplace at Cambridge for almost forty years: major work being carried out on Lockheed C-130 Hercules. On 19 December 1966, XV177, the first RAF Lockheed C-130K, arrived at Cambridge from the USA. Marshall had won the contract to be the UK technical centre for the sixty-six Hercules purchased, carrying out the painting, autopilot installation and production test flying. *(MA)*

Above: In 1969 a major fuel tank corrosion problem was discovered and an extensive programme of repairs to replace some wing centre sections and completely rebuild the outer wings ensued. Here the outer wings can be seen being rebuilt. *(MA)*

Left: As the outer wing replacement programme had produced a wing structure that was unique to the RAF, it was necessary to assess the strength of the wing by carrying out a full stress test to establish the fatigue life of the wing. *(MA)*

As part of the C-130J programme on 19 March 1994, a fifty-hour 'single engine demonstrator' flight programme began to test the Allison AE 2100 engine and Dowty Aerospace R391 propeller. RAF Hercules XV181 was the test vehicle, with the trial engine mounted on the inner port position by Marshall. After completion of the test programme the aircraft returned to normal configuration. *(MA)*

Marshall test pilots on the 'single engine demonstrator' flight deck in 1994. From left to right are: John Blake (Chief Test Pilot), Daz James, Dave Ryding (Flight Test Engineer). *(MA)*

Twenty-five of the original RAF Hercules fleet have now been replaced by twenty-five new Lockheed Martin C-130J Hercules, delivery of which began in 1999. Shown here is a close-up view of the nose of a new C-130J, showing the Allison engines and Dowty six-blade propellers and the positioning of the refuelling probe over the captain's shoulder, unlike the 'classic' Hercules, where it is fitted on the roof over the co-pilot's head. Part of Marshall's work on these airframes was to fit the probes. *(MA)*

Arrival of Lockheed's C-130J demonstrator N4099R at Teversham, this aircraft now serves as 96-8153 with the USAF. *(MA)*

Marshall MATRIX expandable shelter being loaded into a C-130J. These shelters, which expand outwards, have multifarious uses, including hospitals, command posts and communications centres. *(MA)*

... And this shows how the shelter easily expands to provide accommodation. *(MA)*

Marshall has applied its wide experience on the Hercules to those operated by other air forces and also civil operators. Here are some of the company team in front of a Netherlands Air Force example. In the background there is a civil version. The firm has been responsible for more than 600 modifications for the RAF and 201 for foreign operators. *(MA)*

A Swedish Air Force Hercules. *(MA)*

A SFAIR civil Hercules F-GDAQ. *(MA)*

Recently Marshall carried out an extensive upgrade of the South African Air Force's twenty-five-year-old Hercules, which included fitting 'glass' cockpits. This flight deck photograph shows how thorough the work was. *(MA)*

The South African Air Force now has aircraft that are twenty-five years old but fully equipped and structurally sound for a further twenty-five years. One is seen here during an engine test. *(MA)*

Looking east along the Newmarket Road, a sight that will certainly remain familiar to the locals and to all those whose livelihoods depend on the prosperity of the Marshall Group enterprises. *(MA)*

five

Royal Recognition and
Increasing Diversity

Royal Recognition

Arthur Marshall, the company's chairman, was knighted in 1974 for services to the RAF. The firm went on to provide even greater services to the RAF with the invaluable support it gave during the Falklands War.

Vulcans and Buccaneers

At the beginning of the decade Marshall did some work on the Vulcan, a type they had not worked on previously. This was Vulcan B.1 XA903 which had been an Olympus test bed for Concorde at Filton. It was delivered to Cambridge in August 1971, only returning to Filton in February 1972. At Marshall it was fitted with a nacelle under the airframe to carry and test the Rolls-Royce RB199 destined for the Tornado fighter/bomber. The RB199 nacelle represented a starboard installation in the Panavia Tornado fuselage with a fully functional and aerodynamically representative intake and nozzle.

After the Vulcan modifications the firm was also employed in versioning another type to assist with the Tornado development. Two Buccaneers, XT272 and XX897, were modified to carry and evaluate Tornado avionics equipment in flight. In order to accommodate the radar installation, the forward end of the Buccaneer fuselage was altered to accept the Tornado radome and the bomb bay was modified to house test instrumentation and observer equipment. Once completed, the firm managed the test programme before handover to Panavia for Tornado development work at BAe Warton in Lancashire. With all this heavy aircraft activity a further extension of the comparatively short tarmac runway was decided upon and in 1972 it was extended to its present length of 6,447ft.

Vulcan B.1 XA903 operated by Rolls-Royce Filton was delivered to Cambridge in August 1971, where it was fitted with a nacelle under the airframe to carry and test the Rolls-Royce RB199 destined for the Tornado fighter/bomber. *(MA)*

Right above: Buccaneer XT272 at RAE Bedford, which together with XX897 was modified to carry and evaluate Tornado avionics equipment in flight. To accommodate the radar installation, the forward end of the fuselage was altered to accept the Tornado radome and the bomb bay modified to house test instrumentation. Its sister XX897 is now at the Bournemouth Aviation Museum. *(MA)*

Right middle: In the 1950s and 1960s the company was responsible for major modifications and development to many Canberras. In the early 1970s Marshall bought second-hand Canberras for refurbishment and, with BAC's support, received an order from Peruvian Air Force for eleven aircraft in 1973 which were delivered 1975-1978. *(MA)*

Right below: Marshall became a Cessna Citation Service Centre in 1974. The Citation is a popular executive aircraft and Marshall itself operates one. Many owners have used the company's expertise in the refitting and maintaining of their aircraft. *(MA)*

Left above: After the war several Messerschmitt Me-163 rocket fighters were shipped to the UK. 191659 (RAF AM219) was despatched to the College of Aeronautics, Cranfield, in 1947. Except for brief periods of exhibition (e.g. White Waltham, 9 May 1950, where it is pictured), it remained at Cranfield until 1975 when it went to Marshall for refurbishing prior to display at the Royal Scottish Museum of Flight at East Fortune in 1976. It is currently on display there. *(MAP)*

Left middle: Short Belfast G-BFYU (formerly XR367) taking off from Teversham's Runway 23 also carrying 'B' registration G-52-16. (Marshall 'B' registrations all begin G-52.) Heavy Lift bought some of the RAF's redundant Belfasts so Marshall took on design authority from Shorts, which resulted in extensive flight testing order to obtain civil certification. *(MA)*

Cessna Centre

On a different front, the firm became a Cessna Citation Service Centre in 1974 and has remained so ever since. The company has operated three Citations itself as a communications aircraft: G-BCRM, G-BFRM and most recently Citation Bravo G-FIRM. Very recently in April 2003 the company announced plans to set up a charter firm called Marshall Executive Aviation to make better use of its own G-FIRM.

Other activities in the 1970s included designing a Lycoming engine installation and transmission for civil variants of the Westland Lynx and designing ailerons, flaps and slats for the Airbus A310. Likewise Marshall designed, tested and installed an ECM fit in an Indian AF BAE 748. For twenty-five years, from 1974 to 1999, Marshall maintained the Scottish Aviation Bulldogs, operated not only by the locally based University Air Squadron but also at RAF Shawbury in Shropshire.

Following defence cuts in 1976 the RAF's ten-strong fleet of Short Belfast heavy transports were taken out of service. Heavy Lift bought some of them and Marshall took on design authority in order to obtain civil certification. Much military equipment was removed and all avionics updated. As the aircraft had a troublesome stall, the CAA required a stall warner and stick pusher to be installed which involved the company's flight crew carrying out a large number of stalls to thoroughly check the system.

Marshall into Space

The next decade proved immensely busy with all the Hercules activity but even more specialised and indicative of the company's expertise was the Space Sled built for the European Space Agency (ESA). This sled was designed to study the response of the human balance system to non-gravitational acceleration forces and flew 121 orbits in the Space Shuttle *Challenger* in 1985.

In the late 1980s the firm, ever flexible, worked on both modern and ancient jets. At one end of the spectrum they updated the weapons and navigation systems of Royal Jordanian Air Force's Northrop F5s and at the other took over the design authority for the RAF's first jet fighter, the Gloster Meteor, from BAe. And there are a few Meteors still flying in 2003.

For several years Marshall were heavily involved with BAe 146, a four-engined high-wing jet airliner for parts manufacture and later as a completion centre. These airliners were flown 'green' from the BAe factories at Hatfield and Woodford and were finished to customer specification at Cambridge.

To put all these activities into perspective, between 1982 and 1989 the company delivered 1,745 large aircraft and continued in challenging times to produce vehicle bodies.

In 1988 Michael Marshall became High Sheriff of Cambridgeshire and his father stayed on as Chairman until the following year when, at the age of eighty-six, he passed over the role of Chairman to Michael. The Marshall's shareholders elected Sir Arthur as Honorary Life President of the Marshall Group. Michael Marshall continues as Chairman and Chief Executive and has been the Vice-Lord Lieutenant of Cambridgeshire since 1992.

Opposite below: Family, shareholders and directors at the 1979 AGM. Michael Marshall, now Chairman, is standing third from the left and seated in the 1913 Austin 20 are Sir Arthur and his wife, Lady Rosemary Marshall. Marshall became an Austin dealer just after the First World War and remains a dealer with Rover, the successor to Austin to this day. *(MA)*

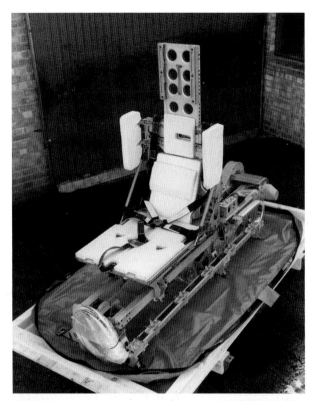

Left: Indicative of the company's expertise was the Space Sled built for the European Space Agency (ESA). This sled was designed to study the response of the human balance system to non-gravitational acceleration forces and flew 121 orbits in the Space Shuttle *Challenger* in 1985. *(MA)*

Below: For rather different altitudes to those operated by the Space Sled, in 1982 rafts were installed in British Airways Chinooks for North Sea operation. *(MA)*

Royal Dutch Air Force Gulfstream touching down at Cambridge. *(MA)*

The firm was appointed Service Centre for all models of Gulfstream in 1960. It was approved by the manufacturer for the complete outfitting of their aircraft often in 'green' (i.e. unfurnished) condition. Seven jet Gulfstreams are visible in this photograph and one Rolls-Royce Dart-powered Gulfstream 1 in the left foreground. *(MA)*

Left: The firm has supplied the Ministry of Defence with more than 80,000 vehicle bodies. Here are Bedford Military MT cabs under construction. *(MA)*

Middle: Variations on a theme. Land Rover Owners' Club 50th Anniversary line-up. Marshall built many of these specialist bodies. *(MA)*

Bottom: A proud line-up of Marshall buses built for MTL Liverpool. *(MA)*

In 1988 the design authority for Britain's first jet fighter, the Gloster Meteor, was transferred to Marshall from BAe. Pictured is Meteor D Mk.16, WK800, which flew at Woomera in Australia for ten years, returning to the UK in 1971 and is now based at RAF Llandbedr. *(MA)*

The Prime Minister, Mrs Thatcher, visited the firm on 27 May 1988. Sir Arthur is on the extreme left and John Huntridge (Managing Director of Motor Group) is in discussion with the Prime Minister. *(MA)*

On Sir Arthur's retirement as Chairman in December 1989, the Aircraft Design Office gave him this sketch, depicting his full and varied career. At the same time he became Honorary Life President of the Marshall Group. *(MA)*

six

The TriStar
Conversions

RAF Lockheed TriStars ZD950 trailing a hose from one of its two-hose drum units. On 2 February 1983, Marshall received a contract to convert nine surplus Lockheed TriStars to long-range high-capacity tanker transports capable of refuelling in the air. This was to replace worn-out Victor tankers and provide additional transport capacity. *(MA)*

Marshall's close association with the Lockheed TriStar began in 1983 when the company was appointed the prime contractor and design authority for the conversion of the six BA L1011-500s to freight and airborne tanker roles.

In 1966, Lockheed started working on what became their first and only jet airliner, the L-1011 TriStar. Though 250 were built, the programme led to Lockheed's withdrawal from the civil aircraft business and total losses to the manufacturer amounting to nearly $2.5 billion. The initial version, which flew in 1968, seated 300 and had full transcontinental capability and was powered by Rolls-Royce RB211s. British Airways was one of the early customers, eventually owning twenty-three, of which six were long-range L1011-500s versions. These had fuselages shortened fore and aft of the wing, increased wingspan and higher payload.

After the Falklands Conflict in 1982 the British Government recognised the need for a long-range high-capacity tanker transport capable of refuelling in the air. This was to replace its worn-out Handley Page Victor tankers and provide additional transport capacity. In September 1982, discussions commenced with the options being either British Caledonian DC-10s or British Airways L-1011s. The former was offered by British Aerospace while Marshall Aerospace offered the latter. In order to fulfil the contract, the company had to seek planning permission from Cambridge City Council to erect another hangar, which is situated on the north-west side of the aerodrome. This became Hangar 17.

TriStar contract

On 2 February 1983, a contract was signed with Marshall's to convert six surplus British Airways Dash 500s. The conversion was no easy task. It was necessary for a new fuel system to be installed as the government required the tankers to carry 45 tons of fuel in four fuel tanks in the fore and three in the aft underfloor cargo bays. These tanks raised the TriStars' fuel capacity to 100,000lbs. Two Flight-Refuelling Hose Drum Units were sited side by side in the aft-most cargo compartment. Another challenge was the installation of a large forward cargo door, which was a first on a TriStar. This 140in by 102in door required the aircraft to be carefully supported and jacked to remove all stresses and loads from the structure, otherwise distortion might have occurred. A large cutout was made in the fuselage which was double the actual size of the door in order to handle the structural loads. The cabin floor was strengthened to allow the carriage of freight pallets. The tanker/freighters can transport up to 100,000lbs freight or 200 passengers.

The first four aircraft – ZD948, ZD950, ZD952 and ZD953 – were initially completed as K1 ('K' for Kerosene) tanker/passenger configuration, lacking the forward cargo door. ZD950, the first conversion made its maiden flight on 9 July 1985. The fifth and six airframes, ZD949 and ZD951, were completed in KC1 ('C' for Cargo) tanker/cargo/passenger configuration. ZD948 and ZD952 later returned to Cambridge for conversion to KC Mk.1 standards with the cargo door.

Initially the tanker TriStars were completed with flight-refuelling probes, but these were not retained as the aircraft carries more than enough fuel for normal operations. There were plans to make them into three-point tankers with underwing pylon refuelling units but this modification was cancelled and the RAF decided to allocate the money to converting more of its VC10s.

A hive of activity in Hangar 17 in 1986. With the need for more tankers and transports the RAF chose Marshall to modify nine surplus TriStars. Here are former British Airways TriStar 500s now carrying military marks as ZD949-51, '953 and N508PA still in Pan Am colours. *(MA)*

In addition to the fitting of fuel tanks and flight-refuelling hose drum units, four of the aircraft also had large freight doors fitted. Here non-destructive loading is taking place to proof-test the worst case loading after these modifications have been made. *(MA)*

FUSELAGE STRUCTURAL TESTING

This is not blurred! This is fuselage structural testing taking place. *(MA)*

Fuselage destressed and supported for installation of the freight door surround. *(MA)*

Left above: TriStar Flight Engineer's station showing the TV screen to view refuelling process.

Right above: With the surround in place the freight door is tested. *(MA)*

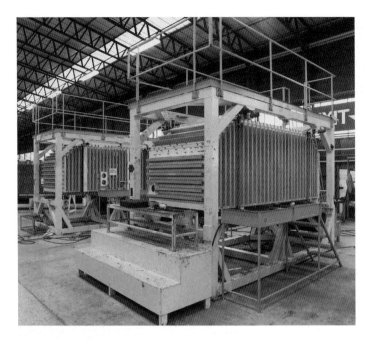

As the TriStar tankers needed more fuel capacity, additional fuel tanks were built and fitted in the cargo bays. *(MA)*

In 1984, the RAF purchased three L-1011-500s from Pan Am, but owing to the detail differences, these could not be converted to the same KC1 configuration. Registered as ZE704 to ZE706 these received minor modifications at Marshall's remaining as standard airliners capable of carrying 250 passengers and were designated as the C Mk.2.

All nine Lockheed TriStars operate with 216 Squadron, which is based at RAF Brize Norton, the home of all the RAF's heavy transports.

Civil freighter conversions

Though Lockheed seriously investigated a cargo conversion of the L1011, it was Marshall Aerospace that really tackled the job. Their confidence and expertise followed from their success with the tanker conversions for the RAF. Marshall selected the L-1011-200 as the ideal model for the conversion, increasing the gross weight from 466,000lbs to 474,000lbs. It was designed to carry up to 23ft by 7ft 4in by 10ft 5in pallets on the main deck, sixteen LD-3 containers weighing up to 36,000lbs in the forward cargo hold, and another eight weighing up to 18,000lbs in the rear hold. The conversion process took eighteen to twenty-two weeks. American International Airways launched the program in July 1994 with an order for three conversions and options on a further five. The airline purchased eight former British Airways TriStars for the purpose, and not long after, three options were confirmed. In early 1995, International Air Leases (IAL) placed an order for three conversions for lease to Arrow Air. Gulf Air L-1011-200s were allocated to this contract. In 1996, well-known commercial aircraft lessor International Lease Finance Corporation (ILFC) ordered a single conversion for Millon Air. The aircraft was provided by LTU. This makes a grand total of ten conversions.

With their proven TriStar expertise Marshall were also able to attract airlines such as Air Canada and British Airways, which required refurbishment programmes on L-1011s.

An aerial view of the airfield with the huge Hangar 17 at the bottom which was built for the TriStar and is one of the largest in Europe. There is a TriStar outside, and elsewhere are BAe 146s and a Gulfstream. *(MA)*

How close can you get? Refuelling in process. *(MA)*

Above: ZD952, a fully converted KC Mk.1 on the Cambridge apron. *(MA)*

Left: The capacious cabin of a TriStar KC Mk.1. *(MA)*

Right: With their clear expertise on the TriStar, Marshall soon took on more work, handling airline examples. BA's G-BHBR served with the airline for ten years before being converted to a freighter by Marshall for American International Airways. *(MA)*

In this beautiful shot a KC Mk.1 is refuelling a RAF Boeing E-3. Marshall also regularly services the Boeing Sentry AEW1s. The TriStar flight-refuelling probes have now been removed, as the aircraft's internal fuel capacity has proved sufficient for operations. *(MA)*

Marshall selected the L-1011-200 as the ideal model for the conversion designed to carry up to twenty-three pallets. American International Airways launched the programme in July 1994 with an order for three conversions. The first conversion N102CK, formerly BA's G-BHBM, first flew August 1995. *(MA)*

TriStar Satellite Launcher conversion

In 1993, Marshall Aerospace took on yet another major conversion programme. On this occasion the work formed part of the NASA Space Programme, namely modifying a former Air Canada L-1011 into a satellite launch platform for the Orbital Sciences Corporation. Previously a NASA B-52 had fulfilled the function but it was now in need of replacement. Modifications to the TriStar included the support and attachment structure underneath the fuselage, a release mechanism, aerodynamic fairings to accommodate the Pegasus satellite, payload air conditioning system, a nitrogen purge system, umbilicals, launch panel operator station, and equipment for testing and launching the satellite. The Pegasus, which is 52ft long and weighs 40,000lbs, has a 22ft wing which fits under the fuselage, with an anhedral tailplane, and the fin is recessed into the unpressurised hydraulic service centre. Christened *Stargazer*, the modified TriStar N140CS successfully completed its maiden flight from Teversham on 12 July 1993. The satellite is launched at an altitude of 38,000ft and can carry both the Hybrid Pegasus and the larger Pegasus XL. The RB211 engines are modified to give ten per cent higher power at the moment of release in order to counter the substantial rearward movement of the centre of gravity.

In 1999, the *Stargazer* returned to Cambridge for modification to carry the joint NASA/Orbital Sciences X-34. This would have served as a test bed for new technologies requiring a high-speed, high-altitude flight environment. However, when NASA cancelled the project in March 2001, the aircraft was placed in storage in the Mojave Desert, Arizona. Recently the programme was re-activated with the Pegasus, and *Stargazer* air-launched a Pegasus XL over the Pacific on 28 June 2003.

In 1993, Marshall was responsible for yet another major conversion programme: modifying a former Air Canada L-1011 into a Pegasus satellite launch platform for the Orbital Sciences Corporation. N140SC *Stargazer* is shown here outside Hangar 17 with some of the team who worked on it. *(MA)*

Modifications to the TriStar included the support and attachment structure underneath the fuselage, a release mechanism, aerodynamic fairings to accommodate the Pegasus satellite, various systems, umbilicals, and equipment for testing and launching it. *(MA)*

The Pegasus, which is 52ft long and weighs 40,000lb, has a 22ft wing, fits under the fuselage, with an anhedral tailplane, and the fin is recessed into the unpressurised hydraulic service centre. *(MA)*

There is also plenty of room for a launch panel operator station in the empty cabin. The satellite is launched at an altitude of 38,000ft and can carry both the Hybrid Pegasus and the larger Pegasus XL. The RB211 engines are modified to give ten per cent higher power at the moment of release in order to counter the substantial rearward movement of the centre of gravity. *(MA)*

Christened *Stargazer*, the modified TriStar N140CS successfully completed its maiden flight from Teversham on 12 July 1993. In 1999, the *Stargazer* returned for modification to carry the 25-tonne joint NASA/Orbital Sciences X-34. However, the project was cancelled in 2001 and the aircraft stored in the Mojave Desert. Recently the programme was re-activated and *Stargazer* air-launched a Pegasus XL over the Pacific on 28 June 2003. *(MA)*

seven

The 1990s and Sir Arthur's Century

Marshall Aerospace stand at the 1992 Farnborough International Air Show. *(MA)*

In the last decade of the twentieth century and into the twenty-first, Marshall continued to demonstrate its pre-eminence as the largest privately-owned British aerospace company. With 1.2 million square feet of hangar space and an untarnished record for high quality of service, the company continues to work on many aircraft both military and civil and from the competing Boeing and Airbus stables.

Dominie refit

In 1964 the RAF ordered twenty Hawker Siddeley 125s (which they christened Dominies) for navigation training and these entered service in 1966. Twenty-five years later the RAF decided to revamp the navigation training flown on their Dominies and awarded a contract to Thorn EMI Electronics as prime contractor, with Marshall carrying out the airframe redesign, modification and test flying. Beginning the following year with XS728, twelve aircraft were sent to Cambridge for a modification programme. This entailed stripping the cabin, removal of two cabin windows, fitting a longer nose for a new radar, and a total avionics refit to make the aircraft suitable for training crews for the Air Force's contemporary aircraft, such as the Tornado.

By way of an assessment of a typical Marshall's year, in 1998 a total of 299 aircraft passed through the works ranging from Boeing 747 to Cessna Citations. Actual aircraft deliveries for 1998 were 140 Gulfstreams, 27 TriStars, 59 Hercules, 35 Cessna Citations, 34 Boeing 747s, 4 DC10s and one each of the Boeing 727, Boeing AWACS Sentry, Airbus A320 and MD11.

Right above: The RAF decided in 1991 to revamp the navigation training flown on their Dominies and awarded a contract to Thorn EMI Electronics and Marshall to revamp the airframe and avionics. Dominie conversion is shown here taking place in the Marshall hangars. *(MA)*

Right middle: Delivery of the first modified Dominie T10. Marshall engineers and RAF pilots are shown here on the Cambridge apron. *(MA)*

Right below: RAF BAE 125 CC.3 ZD703 undergoing static test of DIRCM (Digital Infra-Red Counter Measures) equipment. *(MA)*

British Airways Contract

Between 18 February 1998 and 18 January 2002, over 130 British Airways aircraft passed through the Cambridge facilities. Work carried out ranged from modifications known as Pre-service, Optimum and Satcom, through to full interior reconfigurations. The relationship between Marshall Aerospace and British Airways began with the arrival of 747 G-CIVP for extended crew rest areas and new first class layouts. British Airways then requested Marshall Aerospace to carry out the introduction of the newly launched World Traveller seats. Working around the clock, seven days a week, each aircraft had a turnaround time of twenty days. In fact, the first completed aircraft departed Cambridge and went straight back into service to New York! Straddling the millennium this contract proved very lucrative for Marshall, finally ending as British Airways 747-400, G-CIVF, departed ending a major period of work spanning four years.

Airbus wing test specimens

A recent specialised contract was a 2.1-ton 6-metre-long metal panel produced as part of the enhancement programme for the long-range Airbus A340 aircraft wing makers for Airbus UK. During this testing process the skin of the panel will be stretched up to 12mm in length with the use of enormous hydraulic rams, which will exert a pressure of up to 400 tonnes. In the near future Marshall Aerospace will produce an even larger and more complex test wing section for the new double-decker Airbus A380 which will be over eight metres in length!

In 1997 the first BA Boeing 747 G-CIVP landed at Teversham as part of an initial £8 million contract to modify thirty-two of the 747-400 series of British Airways. *(MA)*

Right above: Extended crew rest areas were part of the BA contract! *(MA)*

Right middle: ... And fully flat Business Class six-foot-reclining bed. *(MA)*

Below: In June 2001 BA took delivery of the 100th 747 to pass through Marshall Aerospace. Another thirty-three 747s passed through during the reminder of 2001 and on 18 January 2002 the last one left. *(MA)*

Marshall has handled many Boeing types – here a trio of Boeing 727s are being refitted, two for executive use and one for Baltic International. *(MA)*

Straight on for Newmarket, turn right for Teversham. The company has worked on many types and this also includes one of the world's classic types the Boeing 707, seen on final approach to Runway 23. *(MA)*

Many BAe 146s and the rebranded RJs (i.e. Regional Jet) were delivered from the BAe factories 'green' to Cambridge for fitting out to customers' requirements. Flying with BAe 'B' registration as G-6-239 is a BAe RJ85. This was delivered to Pelita Air Services of Indonesia as PK-PJJ in January 1993. *(MA)*

After their experience with the TriStar, Marshall also lent their skill to completion work on the Lockheed's rival the Douglas DC-10/McDonnell Douglas MD-11. American Airlines MD-11, registered to the manufacturer as N510MD, suitably squeezed into the hangar in 1990. *(MA)*

'The cream of Manchester'. Just as Marshall built brewer's drays post-war, they are still being built now. *(MA)*

In a similar fashion, the firm is still producing refuse disposal vehicles. *(MA)*

Ambulance bodies being manufactured in one of the hangars on the north side of Newmarket Road. *(MA)*

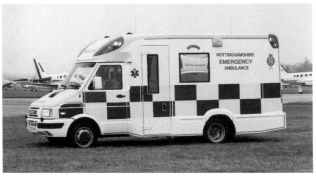

A completed ambulance photographed on the airfield. *(MA)*

In 1994 in alliance with Marshall, Denel of South Africa bid its Rooivalk attack helicopter to win a £2 billion deal to supply helicopter gunships to Britain's forces. It was shown at Farnborough in 1994. Eventually the contract was won by the Westland/Boeing Apache. *(MA)*

The Denel Rooivalk was transported to Cambridge in this Ilyushin 76 and reassembled for Farnborough. *(MA)*

Cambridge Airport receives many unusual and large visitors. Another Russian, an Antonov An-124, is seen here about to touch down at Teversham. *(MA)*

A Russian Antonov An-72 delivering horses to the airfield. With its proximity to Newmarket and the family's close connection with horse-racing, it is appropriate that Teversham should be used. *(MA)*

In late 1994 Airbus A320, then-registered SX-BSV, but which went on to serve with Virgin as EI-VIR. It is commonplace that when aircraft are between owners that their registrations and liveries may not appear to match. (This is also the case with the photograph below.) *(MA)*

In 1994 the RAF adopted an all-black colour scheme for Hawk trainers and the firm was able to further add to the diversity of types handled when it was contracted to repaint some of the type. XX346 is shown here in the paint shop. *(MA)*

Marshall takes very seriously the importance of training to its development and to the wider community. It trains a large number of apprentices and sponsors graduate study, adult re-training and lifelong learning. *(MA)*

Opposite below: Present in 1995 this A320 is seen in American West livery but carrying a Vietnamese registration. *(MA)*

Above: The north side of the Marshall site in the 1970s. It is shown here still with traditional hangars, which were used for aircraft repair and assembly during the war and after. This entailed the aircraft being towed across Newmarket Road to the airfield. In the top right there is a large number of parked military and commercial vehicles. *(MA)*

Below: Nowadays the north side is quite different with the Marshall Car Centre, its major franchises and a combined parts warehouse. Behind the car centre is Marshall Thermo King, which is the main UK Sales and Service Centre for Thermo King vehicle-mounted temperature-control systems. The Marshall Car Centre was opened in 1995 and occupies almost half a mile of prime retail land. *(MA)*

Above: Delta MD-11, N813DE, arriving for cabin outfitting in the summer of 1996. *(MA)*

Right: The Marshall Way. *(Author)*

Below: In 2003 Marshall Motor Group represents fifteen different manufacturers from its Cambridge, Peterborough and Bedford dealerships with a turnover of £300 million. *(MA)*

… And for Boeing

Meanwhile for Airbus rivals Boeing, Marshall are installing crew rest facilities on new aircraft prior to delivery to Alitalia. The first ever Boeing 777 aircraft to be seen at Cambridge arrived on 27 August 2002 directly from the US manufacturer. The arrival of the twinjet, wide-body Boeing aircraft marked the start of a major modification contract for Marshall Aerospace which would see five other B777 aircraft land at the airport, arriving in five-week intervals. Amongst the most impressive recent examples of work in the twenty-first century has been the continuation of the RAF's Boeing Sentry maintenance programme for which the form is Sister Design Authority.

Marks & Spencers!

As part of their bid for the Ministry of Defence's £13 billion Future Strategic Tanker Aircraft programme, the Tanker & Transport Service Company (TTSC) formed by Boeing and BAE SYSTEMS in June 2003 selected Marshall as contractor for the conversion of surplus British Airways Boeing 767s into air-to-air refuelling tankers. The decision is due to be made at the end of 2003.

The first two development aircraft will be modified by Boeing, which is also responsible for conversion design and aircraft certification, but Marshall will reinforce the TTSC team with its experience as prime contractor for earlier conversions of TriStars into tanker/transport configuration for the RAF. The contract will be awarded to the chosen supplier at the end of 2003.

An analyst quoted in the *Daily Express* said, 'You would expect the Boeing/BAE consortium to use Marshall, it's like going to Marks & Spencer for your underwear. They are the people you go to.'

The Motor Group has won numerous accolades over the years and in 2002 the Marshall Land Rover Bedford team came 1st in the UK and 2nd in the World in the International Land Rover Competition held in South Africa.

Marshall Special Vehicles (MSV) continues to make its mark, recently delivering the first Cormorant Communications Vehicles and modular Transportable Surgical Facility to the Army. And Cambridge's famous Addenbrooke's Hospital received its first re-locatable Operating Theatre. As part of the RAF's Airborne Stand-Off Radar (ASTOR) programme Marshall is providing mobile ground stations for high-speed data link with the five Bombadier Global Express aircraft due to go in service in 2005. MSV is likely to play a leading role as a supplier to the MoD in the years to come.

Opposite above: A BA Boeing 767 on approach to Marshall's base for maintenance. If the RAF chooses this type as its new tanker many more former BA examples will visit Teversham. *(MA)*

Opposite below: Just as Marshall worked on Lufthansa Viscounts in the 1950s, forty years on there was work on the German airline's 747s. *(MA)*

In 1998 Bombardier of Canada selected Marshall as a Global Express modification centre. Shown here is an example of a 'green' aircraft ready to be fitted out. *(MA)*

Here is the same Global Express, fitted out and painted with a Marshall 'B' registration G-52-24, awaiting test flying. It later became G-LOBL and is operated by Northern Executive Aviation. *(MA)*

Above: In 1999 Cambridge University Air Squadron moved to RAF Wyton and to mark the occasion there was a gathering of representative aircraft operated between 1940 and 1999; Tiger Moth, Chipmunk and Bulldogs. *(MA)*

Right middle: Over the years a great many aircraft have used Cambridge Airport. Following the crash of a Korean Airlines cargo 747 at Stansted on 23 December 1999, Stansted was closed and there was a large number of diversions to Cambridge including GO 737s. *(MA)*

Right below: The firm has invested £2.5 million in the airport in recent years including updated radar, approach facilities, ILS and a new Control Tower opened in 2000, seen here with five new C-130Js, two C-130K Hercules and a Suckling Airways Dornier 228. *(MA)*

Scot Airways has its permanent base at Cambridge Airport and operates flights from London City to Scottish destinations with its fleet of Dornier 328-100s, though use of the Jaguar is optional. *(MA)*

Above: Sir Arthur Marshall (centre) with members of the family at the unveiling of the plaque in Jesus Lane, Cambridge, in 2000. The tribute states, 'David Gregory Marshall MBE 1873-1942. University Caterer, Sportsman, early pioneer of motoring and flying. Founder of Marshall of Cambridge. This was the site of the main office 1912 to 1939 and continued as a garage until 2000.' *(MA)*

Right: Sir Arthur Marshall and his dog Boris in 2001. Note the B-17 model on the desk which he flew in 1943, and the sketch presented to him in December 1989 outlining his full and varied career (see page 86 for a close-up view). *(MA)*

Opposite middle: After the failure of the Nimrod AEW aircraft the RAF ordered seven Boeing Sentries AEW1s for which Marshall regularly carries out major work as Sister Design Authority. *(MA)*

Opposite below: After maintenance, the Sentry is ready for service again. *(MA)*

Above: Amongst the broad range of Marshall Specialist Vehicles portfolio is the Demountable Rack Off-load Pick-up System (DROPS) vehicle which can be used to transport a number of loads including mobile armoured shelters, and L-band mobile long-range radar spines, which are shown here. *(MA)*

Left: L-band mobile long-range radar spine unloaded and ready for action. *(MA)*

Below: As part of the RAF's Airborne Stand-Off Radar (ASTOR) programme Marshall is providing mobile ground stations for high-speed data link with the five Bombadier Global Express aircraft due to go in service in 2005. *(MA)*

First flight of a Bombardier Global Express configured for the ASTOR programme took place in 2001. The radar installed should provide images of the battlefield at ranges of 100 miles at altitudes of up to 47,000 feet. When in service in the RAF, the Global Expresses will communicate electronic intelligence to the Marshall ground stations. *(Raytheon)*

As part of the firm's continuing work on the interiors and maintenance of McDonnell-Douglas MD-11s it recently handled 'C' checks on five of KLM's airframes turning each one round in seven days. *(MA)*

Conclusion

This company, unlike most other British aerospace firms, is still based in the city in which it was founded and where it is a significant employer. The Marshall Group has more than 3,300 people in its various companies. It is a specialist and a generalist: a rare combination.

Marshall Aerospace, with sales of approximately £110 million per annum, has the breadth of expertise to work on any type or project, covering in-depth design, manufacture, maintenance of military, commercial and business aircraft. It has its own well-equipped airfield and 1.2 million square feet of hangars, which can contain up to three huge 747s, or twelve Hercules or small executive jets or vehicles.

The company owes its continuing existence to its ability to accommodate many aircraft, to accept varying types of work and, unlike so many of today's organisation over-refining its activities, to some very limited 'core' of activity with which it will deal. It has the added strength provided by the Specialist Vehicle Division's work on commercial and military vehicles and the Motor Group, one of the UK's largest privately owned franchised dealer groups. The Motor Group has thirty-five dealerships representing fifteen manufacturers based in East Anglia, Leicester and Reading.

Marshall takes the importance of training very seriously and sees it as crucial to its role as a responsible employer. This can be measured by the statistic that it trains twenty per cent of all UK apprentices, for which it has received awards. It sponsors graduate study, adult re-training and lifelong learning. In 2002 the Marshall Training Centre was named as one of the top Training Providers in the UK by the Adult Learning Inspectorate who stated that 'The quality of their training is a model for others to aspire to'.

As Sir Arthur approaches his 100th birthday in this centenary year of flight, he can feel very proud of the company that bears his name. Not only has it maintained its independence throughout a challenging century but it has had a major part to play in British and world aviation.

Opposite above: On 22 July 2002, Marshall announced a contract to install crew rest facilities on Alitalia's new Boeing 777 prior to delivery. The arrival of the Boeing wide-body twinjet marked the start of a major modification contract which saw five other B777 aircraft land at the airport at five-weekly intervals. *(MA)*

Opposite middle: An artist's impression of the Nimrod MRA4 due to fly in late 2003, for which the firm is making a variety of parts. *(BAE SYSTEMS)*

Opposite below: An artist's impression of Boeing 767 as a RAF flight-refuelling tanker. As part of their bid for the MoD's £13 billion Future Strategic Tanker Aircraft programme, the Tanker & Transport Service Co. (TTSC) selected Marshall in June 2003 as contractor for the conversion of surplus British Airways Boeing 767s into tankers. The decision is due to be made at the end of 2003. *(TTSC)*

Marshall-converted TriStar refuelling a Marshall-converted Hercules. It would be fitting if Marshall were to convert the Boeing 767s as the next RAF tankers when it is remembered how much experience and success the firm has with such major conversions. *(Quinetiq)*

Appendix

Aircraft on which Marshall carried out substantial work or used between 1929 and 2003.

Manufacturer/type	Work done	Dates
Aerospatiale		
Alouette	Camera fit for BBC. Modifications for *Battle of Britain* filming	1968
Dauphine	Modifications	1981
Airbus Industrie		
A310	Design	1978–80
A320	Completion/Modification	1990 to date
A340	Wing spar test section	2003
A380	Test wing section	2003
Airship Beta	Garage assisted when it landed on Jesus Green, Cambridge	1912
Airspeed		
Oxford	Rebuilt hundreds during the war	1940–44
Horsa	Installation of engines in gliders	1945
Ambassador	Freight door conversion	1962–63
Armstrong Whitworth		
Whitley	Repair/rebuild	1940–44
Albemarle	Overhaul/rebuild	1945
Argosy	Roller cargo handling system	1962–63
Avro		
Anson	Wartime maintenance and repair	1939–45
Lancaster	Introduction of night flying equipment	1947
Shackleton	Modification to rear fairing for parachute trials	1961
Vulcan	Modification for Tornado RB199 flying test bed	1971
	Design and maintenance on preserved XH558 for possible flight	1998 to date
BAC		
TSR2	Design work, manufacture flight-refuelling probe and armament installation	1960–64
One-Eleven	Executive interiors for BAC, Horten, Tenneco, Brazilian Air Force. Avionics fit and long-range tanks. Refit	1965–92
Jet Provost	Overhaul/modification for Saudi AF	1967
BAC/Aerospatiale		
Concorde	Design, mock-up for droop nose and visor	1967–70

Manufacturer/type	Work done	Dates
BAE SYSTEMS		
Bulldog	Operation/maintenance at Cambridge and RAF Shawbury	1974–99
Harrier	Design of two-seat trainer cockpit for Indian AF	1979–82
Hawk	Gun installation design for Finnish AF	1979–82
	Repaint for RAF	1994
146/RJ	Design/manufacture components. Executive interiors. Completion	1988 to date
Nimrod	Manufacture of tailplane finlets	2002 to date
Beagle		
Airedale	Installation of Continental engine in place of Lycoming	1960
206	Interior refurbishment	1964
Husky	Modifications	1976
Beech		
Queen Air	Communications aircraft	1968–74
King Air	Communications	1973–74
Bell		
212	Avionics fit for Oman	1976
Blackburn		
Buccaneer	Modified to carry and evaluate Tornado avionics equipment in flight	1973
Boeing		
B–17 Flying Fortress	Wartime maintenance and repair	1942–46
707	Wing pod installation/maintenance	1963–93
727	Servicing	1987–95
747	Design, manufacture of interiors, servicing, design manufacture auxiliary fuel tank	1971 to date
767	Servicing	1990 to date
777	Servicing, installing Crew Rest facilities	2002 to date
Boeing Sentry AEW1	Major servicing	1992 to date
Boeing/Vertol		
Chinook	Raft installation for BA	1982
	Omega installation for Falklands RAF	1982
Bombardier		
Global Express	Completion centre	1998–2002
Bristol		
Brigand	Installation of radar system	1949–50
Britannia	Completion to final delivery standard	1958
Wayfarer	Interior fit/avionics	1960
188	Design of avionics installation	1961
Britten-Norman		
Islander	Painting of 130 aircraft	1969–75
Canadair		
Argonaut	Cabin interior modifications	1960
Cessna		
150/152	Repairs, maintenance, training	1962–89
Citation	Service centre	1974 to date

Manufacturer/type	Work done	Dates
Dassault		
Falcon	Omani paint contract	1985
de Havilland		
Gipsy Moth	Operated for training and wartime rebuild	1929–45
Puss Moth	Charter work	1931–37
Leopard Moth	Charter work	1937
Moth Minor	Trainer	1938–39
Tiger Moth	Trainer	1939–62
Mosquito	Repairs, radar fit, Upkeep bouncing bomb fit	1943–49
Hornet	Development work	1950
Dragon Rapide	Charter work	1950–62
Vampire	Refurbishment and completion work	1950–58
	Fitting ejector seats to 284 Vampires T.11 trainers	
Venom	Final assembly of eighty-four Venoms	1953–56
Comet 1XB	Conversion of one aircraft to high-altitude navigation aircraft	1957–58
Comet 2R	Major conversion of three aircraft to ECM role	1955–57
	Major conversion of one aircraft to ECM role	1961–63
Trident	Design of fuselage components	1959–60
Riley Dove	Installation and certification of turbo-prop variant	1965
de Havilland Canada		
Chipmunk	Maintenance and servicing for Cambridge University Air Squadron and RAF Shawbury	1960–99
Denel		
Rooivalk	Joint Marshall/Denel bid for a £2 billion contract to supply helicopter gunships to Britain's forces	1994
Douglas		
DC-3	Wartime and Berlin Airlift repair centre	1941–64
DC-4	Freighter conversions	1961
DC-6	Freighter conversions	1961
DC-7	Interior modifications	1966
DC-8	Design, installation, certification of spare Avon engine pod	1964
DC-10	Modifications	1988
English Electric		
Canberra	Major modifications, development of B.15 and B.16 variants	1954–65
	Refurbishment for overseas customers	1973–78
Lightning	Design, manufacture of electrical and radio systems F.3	1960–65
General Dynamics		
F-111	Contract to assess instrumented flight trials of armament installation	1967
Gloster		
Gladiator	Wartime repair	1939–40
Meteor	Design authority transferred from BAe in 1988	1988 to date
	Design, development of missile missed-distance indication system	
Grumman/Gulfstream		
Gulfstream	Service and completion centre	1960–2003

Manufacturer/type	Work done	Dates
Handley Page		
Hermes 4	Interior modifications and avionics	1958
Hawker		
Hart	Repairs, maintenance, training	1938–41
Typhoon	Wartime repair	1943–45
Hunter	Servicing at A&AEE Boscombe Down	1987
Hawker Siddeley		
125	Assist Hawker Siddeley with ECM fit on Brazilian AF aircraft	1969
Dominie (RAF 125)	Marshall revamp airframe and avionics	1991–96
RAF Executive 125	ECM on RAF aircraft	1996
748	Indian Air Force ECM fit Interior Refurbishment	1975
	Maintenance	1975
Klemm		
L.25	Training	1930–36
Lockheed		
Neptune	Torpedo adaptor design and fit	1954
Constellation	Radio installation	1961
Electra	Maintenance	1965
Galaxy	Design/build full-scale mock-up of the mainplane and surfaces for USAF Galaxy	1965
Hercules C-130K	UK design, service centre – major modifications for military and civil variants. Including fuselage extension, flight-refuelling receiver / tanker. Refurbishment, resale	1966 to date
TriStar	Design authority for RAF fleet	1983 to date
	Major tanker, freight door conversion	
	Civil freight door conversions	
	Pegasus satellite launch platform conversion	
Hercules C-130J	Completion centre for new Hercules	1998 to date
McDonnell Douglas		
Phantom	Machining of special structural components	1960–87
MD-11	Completion, modification and maintenance centre	1988 to date
Marshall		
MA4	Auster 7 converted for boundary layer experiments	1959–66
Messerschmitt		
Me 163	Refurbishment	1975–76
Miles		
Monospar	Charter work	1936–37
Magister	Wartime trainer	1939–44
Master	Wartime trainer	1939–44
North American		
Harvard	Wartime trainer and repair	1939–45
Northrop		
F5E	Weapon and navigational refit	1987–89

Manufacturer/type	Work done	Dates
Panavia		
Tornado	Design support for Buccaneer avionics trials aircraft and supporting flight trials	1973–75
Percival		
Prentice	Interior fit and radio installation	1949
SAAB		
Viggen	Numerical control manufacture of major machined components	1976–83
Saunders-Roe		
SR 177	Design of major wing structures	1956
Shorts		
Belfast	Design authority, extensive flight test and modifications for CAA certification	1979–81
Sikorsky		
S-61	Modifications for CAA certification	1979–81
Space Shuttle		
Space Sled	Design and manufacture of sled mechanical system for medical research into micro-gravity – 121 earth orbits	1979–85
Supermarine		
Swift	Modification of pre-production aircraft	1952
Vickers		
Viking	Conversion for Queen's Flight and freighter conversions	1953–57
Valetta	Conversions of T3s to T4s with radar fit maintenance	
Varsity	Conversions, servicing	1954–66
Valiant	Design, servicing and many major modifications including Blue Steel trials aircraft	1954–69
	Delegated design authority for electrical system	1956–64
Viscount	Conversions, servicing, repair and completion Weather radar and radio installation	1953–67
V1000	Design work	1954–55
Vanguard	Structural changes to seven of BEA's fleet	1961–62
VC10	Refurbishment of three VC10s used in the test programme to delivery standard	1964
Westland		
Whirlwind	Procedures trainer	1958
Lynx	Design of Lycoming engine installation	1974
Puma	Avionics fit	1981
Wessex	Refurbishment and repaint	1986–87
Gazelle	Refurbishment and repaint	1986–87
Sea King	Strip, corrosion check, refurbish and repaint	1986–87

Note: This list, though extensive and based on a company document, may not cover all types worked on by Marshall. The dates indicate when aircraft types received certain specialist work. Aircraft still in common use may once more enter the Marshall hangars.

Bibliography

Interviews

Sir Arthur Marshall, 10 June 2003
Michael Marshall, 10 June 2003

Books

Aircraft of the Royal Air Force since 1918, Owen Thetford (Putnam, 1995)
Bristol Britannia, David Littlefield (Halsgrove Press, 1992)
British Civil Aircraft Volumes 1 – 3, A.J. Jackson (Putnam, 1988)
British Research and Development Aircraft, Ray Sturtivant (Haynes, 1990)
De Havilland Comet, Martin Painter (Air Britain, 2002)
English Electric Canberra, Ken Delve et al. (Midland Counties Publications, 1992)
Hawker, Bill Gunston (Airworthy Publications, 1996)
A Hell of a Bomb, Stephen Flower (Tempus Publishing, 2002)
Islander 1996, BN Historians (BN Historians, 1996)
Lockheed TriStar, Philip Birtles (Ian Allan, 1999)
The Marshall Story, Sir Arthur Marshall (PSL, 1995)
Tested, Dennis Pasco (Grubb Street, 1999)
Testing Colours, Adrian Balach (Airlife, 1993)
Vickers Valiant, Eric Morgan (Aerofax, 2002)
Vickers Viscount and Vanguard, Peter Davis (Air-Britain, 1981)

Other publications

Marshall Group brochures and newsletters
Marshall Group website
Flight International magazine